The folklore of phantom black dogs is known throughout the British Isles. From the Black Shuck of East Anglia to the Moddy Dhoo of the Isle of Man there are tales of huge spectral hounds 'darker than the night sky' with eyes 'glowing red as burning coals'.

The phantom black dog of British and Irish folklore, which often forewarns of death, is part of a world-wide belief that dogs are sensitive to spirits and the approach of death, and keep watch over the dead and dying. North European and Scandinavian myths dating back to the Iron Age depict dogs as corpse eaters and the guardians of the roads to Hell. Medieval folklore includes a variety of 'Devil dogs' and spectral hounds. Above all, the way people have thought about such ghostly creatures has steadily evolved.

In the last hundred years East Anglia and Dorset have received the greatest attention from folklorists interested in such canine apparitions; this book includes a detailed study of the lore in Norfolk, showing how oral tales become interwoven with published accounts and the 'heritage' of historic places.

But are phantom black dogs nothing more than myths and tales? In this volume there is an assessment of the psychology of phantom black dog sightings. Another chapter quotes emails from various people in America and Canada who have been terrified by phantom black dogs without any prior awareness of such folklore.

The concluding part of this book is a comprehensive annotated bibliography of phantom black dog literature, including listings by geographical area.

This book will appeal to all those interested in folklore, the paranormal and fortean phenomena.

The aim of Heart of Albion's 'Explore' series is to provide accessible introductions to folklore and mythology. Some books provide 'overviews' of quite broad topics, drawing together current academic research with popular beliefs. Other books in the series deal with more specific topics, but still with the aim of providing a wide-ranging introduction to the topic.

Series editor: Bob Trubshaw

Other titles in the 'Explore' series include:

Explore Folklore Bob Trubshaw

Explore Mythology Bob Trubshaw

Explore Green Men Mercia MacDermott

Explore Shamanism Alby Stone

Explore Fairy Traditions Jeremy Harte

Explore Hinduism Bansi Pandit

EXPLORE PHANTOM BLACK DOGS

edited by

Bob Trubshaw

Heart of Albion

EXPLORE PHANTOM BLACK DOGS

edited by Bob Trubshaw

ISBN 1 872883 78 8

Published by
Explore Books
an imprint of
Heart of Albion Press
2 Cross Hill Close, Wymeswold
Loughborough, LE12 6UJ

albion@indigogroup.co.uk

Visit our Web site: www.hoap.co.uk

Printed in England by Booksprint

Dedicated to the memory of Theo Brown (1914–1993)

Contents

List of illustrations

Contributors

Jeremy Harte is a researcher into folklore and archaeology, with a particular interest in sacred space and tales of encounters with the supernatural. His other books include *Cuckoo Pounds and Singing Barrows* (1986), *The Green Man* (2001), and *Explore Fairy Traditions* (2004). He is curator of Bourne Hall Museum in Surrey.

Simon J. Sherwood is a senior lecturer in psychology at the Centre for the Study of Anomalous Psychological Processes (CSAPP), University College Northampton. He has a PhD in psychology from the Koestler Parapsychology Unit, University of Edinburgh. Simon has a Web site about black dog apparitions at http://nli.northampton/ass/psycho-staff/sjs/blackdog.htm

Alby Stone's main interests are the history, archaeology and sociology of religion and associated beliefs and practices; historical linguistics; and the quirks, conceits and follies of the human mind. His books include *Ymir's Flesh: North European creation mythologies* (1997) and *Explore Shamanism* (2003).

Bob Trubshaw has been researching and writing about folklore since the mid-1980s. He is author of several books, including *Explore Folklore* and *Explore Mythology*, plus numerous articles (some of which are online at www.indigogroup.co/edge/ and www.indigogroup.co.uk/foamycustard/).

Jennifer Westwood is a writer and broadcaster on folklore. She is past editor (as Jennifer Chandler) of FLS Books, the imprint of the Folklore Society; and a past editor of the journal *Folklore*. Her books include *Albion: A guide to legendary Britain* (1985), several titles in the Shire 'Gothick' series, *Lost Atlantis* (1997), and *On Pilgrimage* (2003). She has also to many others, among them *The Atlas of Mysterious Places* (1987).

Phantom Black Dogs: an introduction

Bob Trubshaw

Encounters with unfeasibly large dogs, 'darker than the night sky', with eyes the size of saucers and glowing red are likely to be memorable and certainly make good stories. If the sighting is seemingly the portent of a death in a family, the spookiness is enhanced. Little wonder then that, although phantom black dogs may initially appear to be an obscure aspect of folk lore, they seem to generate far more interest than might be expected.

When Katherine Briggs' *Dictionary of British Folk-Tales in the English Language* was published in 1971 she included a lengthy list of phantom black dog sightings. This was probably the first time that so many sightings had appeared outside of specialist publications. Nearly ten years later Janet and Colin Bord undoubtedly raised awareness of the geographically wide-ranging tales further by devoting a chapter of *Alien Animals* to 'Mysterious black dogs'.

In this chapter the Bords note that the folklore of phantom black dogs seems to arise from long-ago myths yet, at the same time, such spectres are still being seen, often by people who seemingly have no prior awareness of relevant lore or myths (Bord and Bord 1980: 109). As with David Hufford's classic study of specific forms of sleep paralysis and the Old Hag phenomena in Newfoundland (Hufford 1982) we seem to be walking on the cracks between a 'phenomenon' and its folkloric echoes. Black dog lore should be regarded neither as 'just folklore' nor 'explained away' as some psychological aberration.

In other words an anomalous psychological phenomena (perhaps some kind of brief temporal lobe dissociation, as discussed in Simon Sherwood's contribution to this book) is 'perceived' according to culturally-specific lore. Such culturally-specific perceptions of anomalous phenomena mean that visions of the Virgin Mary tend to be seen in Catholic cultures whereas Protestant ones tend to see ghosts, and Japanese ghosts tend to be different from British ones. Perhaps phantom black dogs are essentially culturally-specific spontaneous psychological responses that might arise in any society familiar with large dogs.

Despite the psychological aspects of phantom black dogs, we most often encounter them as examples of folklore. As is inevitable with modern day tales and legends, lore which was once transmitted mostly during face-to-face conversations is now kept alive in numerous written versions which generate both concise summaries and more inventive elaborations. Both the summaries and elaborations may introduce misunderstandings, errors and conflations with other similar tales. The popularity of black dog tales means that they provide excellent examples of how lore keeps reappearing in newspaper articles and a wide range of other popular publications.

Indeed the sheer quantity of published references to phantom black dogs makes a comprehensive bibliography essential. Thankfully Jeremy Harte has applied himself to this task and one of the key contributions to this book is his annotated catalogue of black dog lore in England. He has arranged the references three ways: county-by-county, then by motif and then chronologically.

The geographical listing reveals that all counties of England except Middlesex and Rutland have reported sightings of phantom black dogs. Jeremy's listing supports the opinion that phantom black dogs are regarded as especially prevalent in 'East Anglia, the northern counties, and the south-west, and occur sporadically elsewhere' (Simpson and Roud 2000: 25). However the greater number of sightings in specific areas is partly a result of researchers, such as Theo Brown in the south-west, actively seeking such tales, and of specific examples (such as Bungay and Blythburgh) becoming locally well-known, thereby prompting more interest and awareness of similar tales in the area. As ever, we must suspect that the distribution of examples is most closely correlated with distribution of active research and with the publicity given to such tales rather than with any underlying variation in the frequency of such accounts.

Jeremy's chronological list starts in 1803. This may seem a surprisingly late date, especially as medieval lore speaks of 'Devil dogs' and a range of shape-shifting phantoms that sometimes took on the appearance of black dogs. But, as Jeremy discusses in the chapter that opens this book, the concept of 'phantom black dogs' is one invented by folklorists and once diverse spectres have been 'adjusted' to fit within this concept. By looking at the way folklorists have studied phantom black dogs and related phenomena, this opening chapter both successfully sets the stage for the subsequent chapters and also provides a survey of the study of the lore.

However, as already noted, we should not think of phantom black dogs as being 'nothing but' folklore. Rather we should also see them also as psychological phenomena. Simon Sherwood's chapter discusses the psychological and parapsychological approaches to related phenomena and provides a detailed insight into the non-folkloric way of approaching the enigma of phantom black dogs.

Alby Stone then looks at the appearance of black dogs in Indo-European mythology, especially their role as guides to and guardians of the underworld. The phantom black dogs of recent centuries, often regarded as portents of death, seem to be the latest manifestations of 'hell hounds' who have even closer associations with death and the afterlife.

Jennifer Westwood's detailed study of Norfolk black dogs – the Black Shuck – reveals firstly how specific locations once had their related lore and secondly how recent written versions of such lore have led to the legends becoming both better known but also less distinctive. Jennifer's contribution confirms that, despite the generalised nature of the discussions in other chapters of this book, black dog lore is something which must be studied in detail in a specific locality, even if these days the research is more about tracking down published versions of the lore than talking to elderly informants.

In contrast to East Anglia, there are relatively few reported sightings of phantom black dogs from the Americas, and such lore as has been published is mostly in rather obscure books. Therefore my curiosity was greatly awakened when, as a result of two articles about black dogs being published on the Web (Trubshaw 1994a; 1994b), I began to receive emails from the New World reporting sightings of phantom black dogs by people who seemingly had no awareness of the folklore. My interest was two-fold. Firstly, these were apparently spontaneous experiences of the black dog phenomenon. Secondly, here were first-hand accounts of 'folkloric' experiences that were now in written form without any intervening 'collector' to edit, however subtly, the accounts. My contribution to this book therefore publishes these reports for the first time and attempts to make a provisional analysis of the extent to which phantom black dog lore has – or has not – been disseminated in the Americas.

I would like to thank all the authors for their contributions. In editing I have looked mostly for consistency within each chapter and have not necessarily sought consistency of style throughout all chapters. The only exception is with the citation of references as all contributions share the same list of references, printed towards the end of the book.

As Jeremy discusses in more detail, one person in particular is especially associated with the study of phantom black dogs – Theo Brown. During 1960s and 70s she exhaustively recorded examples of phantom black dogs, especially in Devon. She had written a full-length book about black dog lore in 1963 but this was never published. The manuscript – together with many of her other notes – survives in the University of Exeter Library. Her only published work on this topic was restricted to articles in *Folklore* and *Lore and Language*; a chapter in *Animals in Folklore* (Brown 1958, 1964; 1978b); and reports of Devon examples in the *Transactions of the Devonshire Association* (Brown 1955; 1959; 1964; 1978a; 1983; 1985; 1988).

Unusually for her generation Theo was willing to bridge the great divide that then separated folklorists from parapsychologists. 'Theo's outlook embraced the whole spectrum – for spectrum we now recognise it to be – from the veridical "perception" at one end to the fully developed legend at the other. She was a member of the Society for Psychical Research for many years, and was daring enough indeed to deliver a lecture there in 1973, when she was given a sympathetic hearing by an audience to whom folklore was usually anathema.' (Blacker 2001: 252–3)

As Theo Brown's book on black dogs never made it into print there has previously not been a title devoted to this topic. It therefore seems most appropriate that this book is dedicated to her memory.

Early in 2005, after this book had reached page proof stage, a Web site devoted to phantom black dogs in Norfolk, Suffolk and Essex (www.shuckland.co.uk/) appeared. This has been created by Mike Burgess and is a detailed catalogue of the East Anglian lore, forming a useful adjunct to this book.

Black Dog Studies

Jeremy Harte

A lonely road, a black shape seen against the dark, fiery eyes, a sudden disappearance; encounters with a spectral dog seem not to have changed much over the centuries. Seven hundred years ago that enterprising figure, Robert fitz Art, appeared to Alice Kyteler as a shaggy black dog, while a quick search of the Internet will find examples of much the same thing from this year or the last. The headless horseman rides no more, and the phantom funeral has gone to its long rest, but the Black Dog is still very much with us.

Like some other canine pedigrees, however, this one repays closer examination. Though consistent in appearance, supernatural dogs can vary widely in character; after all, Robert was a devil, not a ghost. Most of the early stories have a whiff of sulphur about them, and as late as the 1770s, the mastiff dog that appeared to Mr D.W. of Pembrokeshire was identified as 'one of the infernal hounds of hell' (Kittredge 1929: 176–7; Jones 2003: 125). The Black Dog of Newgate, a well-loved London horror of the seventeenth century, was more ghostly, but barguests, padfoots and other terrors of the northern night continued for many years to occupy an ambiguous status, part animal, part spectre, and part fiend (Wright 1898: 1.164, 2.770, 4.406).

In fact, it was the Victorians who first identified the figure that we call the Black Dog. This process began with E.S. Taylor and T.T. Wilkinson, writing about their local ghosts for *Notes & Queries* (then the standard journal of folklore) in 1850. Coming from separate parts of the country, they described the shuck of Norfolk and the trash or skriker of Lancashire in ways that were obviously similar. Fourteen years later, a contributor to Chambers' *Book of Days* could say, with the air of one stating a received truth, 'in almost every county there is a popular belief in a spectral dog, which, although slightly varying in appearance in different parts, always bears the same general characteristics. It is described as large, shaggy, and black, with long ears and tail'

The black dog of Newgate prison, London. Said to date from C13 when prisoners ate a magician. Reproduced by kind permission of Fortean Picture Library.

(Chambers 1864: 2.433). Indeed, this was more than belief; he himself had spoken to people in Hertfordshire and Dorset who had seen the dogs.

The informant from Dorset was 'a respectable intelligent woman', which rather surprised the anonymous correspondent, since he wanted to set her experience down as a delusion. Given the temper of the times, what else could he think? It was one thing for a folklorist to quote the words of those who had encountered Black Dogs; Alfred Easther's record of Almondbury people who had seen the padfoot is a model of direct reporting (1883: xxiii–iv). These apparitions 'were something more than a name... Whether or not we believe in the *story*, we *do* believe in the perfect honesty of those we got it from', said C.C. Robinson (1862: 380). But all the Victorian folklorists suffered from a kind of cognitive dissonance when they came to interpret this evidence. Sabine Baring-Gould knew more than most about the subject. He had lived among communities familiar with the padfoot of Leeds and the phantom dogs of rural Devon; he had experienced the supernatural more than once himself. But when he came to write about the Black Dog, it was as a survival of prehistoric ideas in the popular mind, and not as a lived reality (1892: 16–17). Was the Black Dog a vestige of foundation sacrifice? Did it belong with the Teutonic storm-hounds of the Wild Hunt? English folklorists happily mulled over these and other themes, quoting and requoting an increasingly standardised body of texts, but they never made much enquiry into the actual experience of Black Dogs.

Meanwhile in the living tradition, views about the supernatural had changed. At the beginning of the nineteenth century, most apparitions could be expected to take more than one form. In Yorkshire, the Holden Rag was seen 'sometimes in the form of a great black dog, and at other times as a rag of white linen on a thorn'; Durham keelmen saw the Hylton Lane Brag in 'the form of a dog, at other times that of a calf, at other times again, that of a Galloway and occasionally that of a woman'; at Kirton in Lindsey, something appeared that was 'like a dog, then like a fox with a bushy tail, and then a woman in white with blood stains on her dress' (Wilkinson 1904–5: 4–5; Brockie 1886: 54–5; Miller 1984: 130).

But by 1900 outré demons of this kind were not so common. Apparitions tended to take one form, and stick to it. The barguest of Yorkshire, on its earlier appearances, had been a shapeless polymorphic horror (Gutch 1901: 125–8). By the 1870s it was an apparition 'taking usually the form of a big black dog with saucer eyes', and in later references it is unequivocally a Black Dog (Moorman 1916: 37). Behind the standard phrases which describe these apparitions – 'as large as a donkey', 'as big as a calf', 'shaggy as a bear' – there are traces of earlier stories in which they had actually been bears, calves and donkeys. When the Leeds carrier saw a padfoot 'rolling along the ground before her, like a woolpack', it is not certain whether the dog had turned into a bale of wool, or was just behaving like one (Henderson 1879: 273–4).

Clearly the answer lay in a better collection of the evidence. But nobody went systematically looking for this until 1925, when Barbara Carbonell began talking to people in her home district of north Devon. Carbonell was not a regular folklorist, but she had been a member of the original Straight Track Club, and was following a string of Black Dog sightings between Copplestone and Torrington out of interest in the ley theory of Alfred Watkins. In fact the dog seemed to prefer the old coaching road to any of Watkins' intangible, cross-country alignments; but in searching for him, Carbonell hit a rich seam of local lore. There was the tall, silent dog which walked by the miller's waggon, year after year; the dog that noisily knocked down a schoolhouse wall every night, though it was all still there in the morning; even the dog which appeared to her own daughter as she drove home one night (Chope 1927: 161; Day 1958: 204–17; Harte 1995).

Carbonell may have been dissatisfied with her results, since they were left unpublished for some thirty years; meanwhile the focus of the subject had shifted to the other side of the country, where Ethel Rudkin was collecting stories from Lincolnshire. Rudkin's paper on the Black Dog, published by *Folk-Lore* in 1938, was the first regional study of the subject. In 1975 she met Keith Miller, who was later to publish his own interviews with people who had seen Black Dogs. Between them they knew of at least 77 locations for the apparition, making Lincolnshire one of the most haunted counties in England (Rudkin 1938; Rudkin 1955; Miller 1984).

Rudkin and Miller both published distribution maps of these findings, which add a comforting air of certitude to their research; here, it seems, the intangible has been given form at last, and pinned to the chart. But the feeling of certainty fades as soon as broader comparisons are made. On a national scale, the distribution of Black Dogs reflects nothing about the phenomenon, only the presence of people who are interested in it. Ted Waring in Dorset, Barbara Spooner in Cornwall, Kathleen Wiltshire and Katy Jordan in Wiltshire – they all created a corpus of sightings for counties where previously little or nothing had been known. In East Anglia the dog features in many antiquarian studies, and writers (most recently Ivan Bunn and Jennifer Westwood) have winnowed through these to produce a picture of him. In Yorkshire, by contrast, there are just as many references in the early literature, but no researcher has ever brought these together into a single study.

So even our first steps in the study of Black Dogs – attempts to say what they are like, and where they have been seen – do not seem as easy as we thought. Definitions will vary from one writer to another, which is why we are often assured that Black Dogs can be white. This is not as daft as it sounds, since at places like Eresby and Alfriston white dogs are seen along the local roads, haunting the scene of a tragedy and portending death; all the usual themes of the literature (Welby 1934–5; Beckett 1909: 215–9). Then we have dogs of a more unusual cast – one with white hair in punk spikes, and another which turned white and rose up in the air (Bord and Bord 1987: 47; Turner 1993: 157). We have already met with Black Dogs in the form of donkeys and bears. Where does it all end?

Perhaps there is no reliable touchstone by which we can define a Black Dog. Each story links with other stories, each experience with others of a similar kind, in a potentially infinite web of connections.

We agree, more or less, on what a Black Dog is, but over time this consensus will change, because both cultural ideas and supernatural experiences will add or take away images from the shared stock of motifs.

It was the imagery of the Black Dog which inspired Theo Brown (1914–93), a folklorist who lived for many years at Postbridge on Dartmoor. Postbridge was a working village, not very picturesque or attractive to outsiders, and this suited her unsentimental, no-nonsense attitude to folklore. The same attitude coloured her thoughts on the supernatural – ghosts were as real as Dartmoor mist, and their relations with the human world could be studied like any other feature of local life. When she returned to Devon after the war, Brown was already interested in the Black Dog. In her first paper on the subject, she cited Margaret Murray as an influence (Brown 1958: 175). Other studies followed over the next twenty years, and a draft was prepared for the press in 1963, but returned by the publishers. In all, she worked on Black Dogs for fifty years – the pattern of a scholar who has one classic book inside them, but never gets round to writing it (Blacker 2001).

It was not just procrastination. Brown, who knew more about Black Dogs than anyone before or since, was searching for the right language and ideas to interpret them, and this could not be done through conventional methods of folklore. Another book – the one which Brown was trying *not* to write – came out in 1959; this was Barbara Woods' *The Devil in Dog Form*. It is a painstaking catalogue, which works its way by type and motif through every apparition of a dog in Europe, and Woods takes it for granted that every account is a fiction taken from a genre of local legends. Why explain, when you can classify?

When it came to English material, Wood found it rather disappointing, there was so little that could be called a story. True, there was the Black Dog of Uplyme, who appeared in the corner of a farmer's cottage for many nights until in a fit of drunken resentment he struck out at it. The blow struck empty air, for the dog had vanished; but where the farmer's stick cracked against the wall, the plaster broke, and out tumbled a hoard of ancient golden coins (Chambers 1864: 2.434; Larwood and Hotten 1866: 193). A good story – but what they call an oecotype, a unique local variant, found nowhere else.

The Black Dogs of England had saucer eyes, just like the three hounds in Hans Christian Andersen's 'The Tinder Box', but there the resemblance ended, for there was nothing to compare with the detailed Danish and German lore of treasure-guarding black dogs. It is not that people did not know any stories. A good old-fashioned tale of warning, 'The Devil Among the Card-Players', is passed on in many places; in continental versions the Devil often appears in the form of a Black Dog, but hardly ever in this country (Woods 1959: 68; but see Parke 1963: 486). By the nineteenth century, indeed, people saw much less of the Devil than their forebears had. True, there was a tradition that midsummer bonfires and wrestling had taken place around an old barrow at Whiteborough Down in Cornwall, until an evil-looking black dog was seen in the crowd, and after that no-one could go to the wrestling without getting hurt (Brand 1849: 1.318–9). But the Devil was on the way out. His last bow came at Longbridge Deverell in Wiltshire, when he appeared in dog shape to break up the annual Palm Sunday gathering. ' "Sum'at was there, anyhow", and they all ran away' (Powell 1901: 74).

Not that the Black Dogs of England lacked variety. The selection of narratives in Katharine Briggs' great *Dictionary of British Folk-Tales* shows the range of storytelling (Briggs 1971: B1.3–19; cf. Williams 1994, 1995). At Martinhoe the wicked Sir Robert Chichester came again as a Black Dog in a flaming car drawn by four elephants (Halliday 1954: 110). Nearby, on the road to Tavistock, Lady Howard does penance for the murder of four husbands as she rides each night in a coach of bones, preceded by a one-eyed hound (Brown 1959: 39). In Northumberland, the unquiet spirit of the avaricious Lady Fenwick appears as a Black Dog ('Q' 1910–11: 391). Many other apparitions walk accompanied by a dog; these, too, have been considered part of the Black Dog tradition (Wiltshire 1973).

It was the outstandingly wicked and rich who came again in dog form, though whenever there had been a murder, a suicide or an untimely death, the Black Dog was said to walk. These were not anybody's ghost, in the ordinary sense; Ethel Rudkin catches the allusive sense of tradition when she says that one of her apparitions was 'connected in the local mind with a woman who drowned herself' (Rudkin 1938: 121). Untimely death itself, breaking the proper thread of life, is marked by the sign of the dog, which appears indifferently at the place where someone was murdered or at the gallows where the murderer swung (Miller 1984: 135). The dog may bear witness to a bad death, or even to a failure to follow proper funeral rites. A Black Dog ran at Budleigh Hill because a coffin had cracked open there on its way to the churchyard (Thornton 1897: 20–2).

Significantly, Theo Brown's two main papers on the subject, and her contribution to Patricia Dale-Green's *Dog*, tried to move on from the minutiae of Black Dog lore to a broader interpretation. She wrote of Nehalennia, Nodens and Nemetona, and of the mythical character of the dog in general – its howling, guardianship, scavenging of bodies and so on (Brown 1958; Dale-Green 1966: 47–84; Brown 1978b). The actual encounter with a Black Dog was a kind of dream, to be interpreted through a study of the symbols latent in it. Her method was closely based on Jung's theory of archetypes, and had its weaknesses as well as its strengths.

Brown sought to explain encounters with Black Dogs through their symbolic content. But she did not explain why a dog should be encountered at a particular place and time. This would have meant looking at the Black Dog as a natural phenomenon, and the folklorists were not yet ready for this. Instead, the impetus of study was taken up by a small group of researchers associated with the newly founded *Fortean Times*. Writing in the early 1970s, they accepted that Black Dogs were quasi-physical; for the duration of the sighting they could be seen, heard and perhaps touched, but afterwards they disappeared into some other realm of being. It was as if a dog shape was being mapped onto a natural phenomenon, perhaps the still unexplained phenomenon of ball lightning (Bord 1974; Moore 1976; Michell and Rickard 1977: 122–3; cf. Rogers 1994: 177–9). If sightings occurred at churchyards, crossroads, and watercourses, then this could be linked with the mysterious energies which seemed to emanate from these places.

How long had this been going on? In 1577 the apparition of a black dog was seen in the church of Bungay as lightning struck the building. Since Victorian times, this incident has been linked with the lore of Black Shuck, so it now seems natural to think that he himself visited the town on that August afternoon. People certainly like the idea, which is why Bungay now has a shop, football team, running club and marathon with the Black Dog logo (Sherwood 2002c: 5). But the connection seems to exist only for antiquaries and forteans – it is not in the original sources – and the storm-demon owes much to the imagination of a pious Elizabethan journalist (Reeve 1988: 45); see Chapter 5 in this volume.

If the Black Dog of Bungay was only a fiction, what of those that people actually met? In what sense could they be real? Stephen Jenkins thought that they were embodied projections, akin to the *tulpas* of

Vajrayana teaching; and as he was one of the few people to have hands-on experience of both Black Dogs and Tibetan esotericism, his views should carry some weight (Jenkins 1977: 177). Jenkins, as it happened, was not the only scholar of the Black Dog to encounter his subject; Ethel Rudkin and Kathleen Wiltshire also had sightings (Brown 1958: 179; Wiltshire 1984: 20).

The tulpoid theory was attractive, for it could also make sense of the alien big cats which had stalked the British countryside from the 1970s onwards. These were substantial enough to leave footprints and torn carcases, but they were never caught, which left the field open to a more esoteric explanation. Di Francis, for whom the Surrey puma and its relatives were actual zoological specimens of a British wild cat, turned the argument the other way round, and suggested that the classic Black Dog encounter was simply a misunderstood meeting with a large cat (Francis 1983: 116–128; see also Watson 1997). She had to select the right sightings to fit this argument, just as Michell and Rickard had for theirs; occasions in which the Black Dog exploded in a ball of fire, so supportive of the fortean case, were tacitly left out of the cryptozoological version. Meanwhile Black Dog sightings continued through the 80s and 90s at much the usual rate, regardless of the existence (or otherwise) of British big cats.

Janet Bord's chapter in *Alien Animals* was the most comprehensive survey of the literature so far, with Graham McEwan's *Mystery Animals* following closely after (Bord and Bord 1980: 77–111; McEwan 1986: 119–149). Among this wealth of evidence, it was tempting to pick that which suited the mood of the times; thus, a link with ancient sites was proposed on the basis of two or three accounts in which the dog appeared by a road leading past some barrows, together with Mr D.W.'s encounter by some standing stones and the Devil's apparition on Whiteborough Down. Maybe these represent a genuine theme, but the evidence seems a little thin.

For the Victorian folklorists, accounts of Black Dogs had been no more than traditions. Attempting to redress the balance, the early forteans took to treating every story as a literal, factual account. If the Black Dog breathed fire, or spread itself out like a quilt and floated off over the trees – well, that just went to prove what a weird place the world was. There were dissenting voices. Jerome Clark, in his perceptive survey of the literature on anomalies, wondered why Black Dog stories were not sifted with the same care that was given to UFO sightings (Clark 1993: 398–400). Too many stories have somebody's grandfather for credentials – sometimes their grandfather's grandfather (Lofthouse 1976: 44). Even personal evidence has its problems. In 1780 Samuel Drew was out with some friends, poaching on the downs above St Blazey. He heard a noise like the clatter of hoofs, and saw an animal like a bear or dog, with glowing eyes, that walked through a closed gate. 'Had it not been for the unearthly lustre of its eyes, and its passing through the gate as it did, there would be no reason to suppose it anything more than an animal perhaps escaped from a menagerie. That it did pass through the gate without pause or hesitation I am perfectly clear' (Drew 1861: 33–5). This is a careful, first-hand account. Nevertheless, Samuel Drew only told it to his son some forty years after the event, when memory might well be unreliable, and all the other witnesses were dead.

Besides, there are problems with definition. Just as it is hard, in some cases, to say whether an apparition is or is not a Black Dog, so there are different views over which mental states count as genuinely anomalous. Theo Brown, from her Jungian standpoint, regarded dreams and paranormal encounters as two aspects of the same thing. She also included things seen in hypnagogic states – the hallucinatory state between sleeping and waking – along with the kind of apparitions that happen in a normal state of consciousness. More recently, Simon Sherwood has argued along the same lines (Brown 1983; Sherwood 2000c: 229; Sherwood 2002a: 3; see Chapter 3 in this volume. Some writers are careful to cross off ghosts of ordinary household dogs from their list; others regard the behaviour of actual dogs, under the right circumstances, as a key to whole business (Huff 2002; Brown 1962; Sherwood 2000d). In either case, very knowledgeable conclusions can be drawn, but it is not clear if they are reflecting the phenomenon itself or just a particular researcher's selection of data from it.

In the end, Brown concluded that debate over whether the Black Dog was subjective or objective would lead nowhere (1958: 188). A different way of thinking was needed, one which paid attention to the story of a sighting without forever trying to pin it down to natural or supernatural origins. Like much of the discourse theory of the 1990s, this took its cue from France. Mysterious big cats had flourished south of the Channel, so that both Michel Meurger and Véronique Campion-Vincent were able to write monographs on the subject. Not for them the fuzzy photos and footprint casts of the English pragmatists; they wanted to discuss, not what big cats were, but what they meant. Encounters with Black Dogs could be treated in much the same way, and this approach was taken by Michael Goss, one of the few writers at home in both folklore and fortean studies. Thus he could juxtapose the dog seen at midnight by three Essex teenagers with an episode in *Far from the Madding Crowd*, not because either account was false or true, but because both said something about the social meaning of tradition (Goss 1992a; Goss 1992b; cf. McGrory 1995). In this reading, the presence of Black Dogs at water and churchyards retained its significance, as it had for earlier forteans, but not as a consequence of earth energy at ancient sites. Instead, bridges and the grave were liminal sites, places of passing over from one reality to another (Trubshaw 1994b; Devereux 2001: 91, 108, 156–9). And the dog belonged to them because, as in so many mythologies, he was a guide to the dead, or a guardian for their kingdom (Leach 1961:135-146); see Chapter 4 in this volume.

The psychosocial approach drew attention to other aspects of encounters with Black Dogs – in particular, to the circumstances of the people who saw them. Samuel Drew had already been thinking on these lines, two centuries before. 'If it be enquired why such a creature was sent, or permitted to appear to us, a satisfactory answer can scarcely be given. With reference to myself, I might observe, that I was at this time forming acquaintances, and contracting habits, of a most pernicious kind' – as, indeed, the Essex teenagers may have been. We have moral Black Dogs which frighten drunkards or card-players into better behaviour, and remorseless ones which punish an affront given to them, or any attempt to disbelieve in their existence. In Yorkshire towns they imposed a virtual curfew: 'nothing could more effectively clear the streets by night than the report that 't' guy-trash was out' (Dawson 1882: 389).

Different communities had different Black Dogs, and this is true above all of the secret community of children. Take the district of Bent Ing outside Bradford in the 1890s, where half a dozen girls sat in a row on the bridge, waiting for the dark to fall so that they can terrify each other with stories about the Bloody Tongue. He was 'a great dog, with staring red eyes, a tail as big as the branch of a tree, and a lolling tongue that dripped blood. When he drank from the beck the water ran red right past the bridge' (Southwart 1923: 26–8). Nobody had ever seen him – apart from one girl, but she saw him in the shadows every night, so that didn't count. He lived only as a rumour legend, but in the hands of a less sensitive writer, Bloody Tongue would have been recorded as just another instance of the Black Dog phenomenon.

Sometimes children took the opportunity to frighten their younger brothers and sisters, shouting "Darley'll get 'ee!" as they did in Cornwall (Spooner 1925–30a: 26). Sometimes they were on the receiving end of the adult imagination. Charles Dickens was frightened witless by his nurse with tales of a Black Dog; so was Charlotte Brontë, if the account in *Jane Eyre* is autobiographical (Dickens 1861: 234; Brontë 1847). And the Jesuit schools inspired a wholesome terror in pupils by telling how one of the fathers, going the rounds of the dormitory at night, paused to comfort a distressed and sleepless young sinner, but to no effect; and as he returned, a black dog slipped past him, brushing his cassock, and all at once disappeared. The boy was found dead in the morning. This story was so well known that it featured in a 1910 paper on intimidation in education (Woods 1959: 106). James Joyce must have heard it at Clongowes, for it surfaces in the childhood chapter of *Portrait of the Artist as a Young Man*. 'The prefect's shoes went away. Where? Down the staircase and along the corridors or to his room at the end? He saw the dark. Was it true about the black dog that walked there at night with eyes as big as carriage-lamps? They said it was the ghost of a murderer. A long shiver of fear flowed over his body'.

Not all Black Dogs are as terrifying as this, but any encounter with them stirs the feelings. Sometimes, as in a dream, this emotional content is only loosely keyed in to the apparent details of what is seen. When popular tradition rings the changes on the ghostly theme, we are to understand the different motifs as so much dramatic statement, not as literal description. Thus we hear of Black Dogs which have no heads while barking furiously; of headless dogs with glowing eyes; and, perhaps the *ne plus ultra* in this field, a black headless dog that emerges from a drain, carrying his head under his arm (Hardwick 1872: 172; 'T.D.P.' 1864; Hood *et al* 1926: 369).

In all these stories, the dog functions as a sign; the motifs pile up, regardless of their redundancy or contradiction. A sign of what? Often the apparition of the dog comes before death, though this can be understood in many different ways. Sometimes death is the consequence of hitting the dog or shouting at it; sometimes the shock of seeing the dog is enough to bring on death, as it did in fiction for Sir Charles Baskerville; but most often the dog is an omen or portent of death (Woods 1959: 100–2). In an earlier, more hierarchical society he appeared to announce the death of the squire (Henderson 1879: 275; Cudworth 1886: 172). In a fishing community, the Black Dog might be a sign of an impending storm at sea; in a mining village, of a pit disaster ('T.D.P.' 1864; Reeve 1988: 67; Daniel 1973: 46; Leese 1989: 23). In our more family-based society, he announces the death of a close relative (e.g. Taylor 1990).

It is the same motif, and yet not the same; the dog has kept pace with our cultural expectations. This is also true of his appearance and behaviour. Early informants liked to pile on the terrors when they described a sighting. 'The dog was the strangest looking creature I ever beheld... very gaunt, shaggy, with long ears and tail, eyes like balls of fire, and large long teeth, for he opened his mouth and seemed to grin at us. He looked more like a fiend than a dog' (Chambers 1864: 2.434). But in the twentieth century, these terrors fade away. In Wiltshire, where Katy Jordan has recorded more recent sightings, the Black Dogs are just like any other dog until they vanish or pass through a solid hedge (Jordan 2000: 173–183). Wonder is provoked, not by sulphurous flames, but by an inexplicable creepy feeling, or by puzzled memories of the phantom's soundless tread. In other words, the sense of the supernatural has been internalised; it no longer depends on melodramatic stage props of fire and noise, but on inward feelings of spookiness.

We no longer believe in a real, personal, brimstone Devil, and so Black Dogs are becoming less fiendish. The old-style dog was an evil spirit, like the one from Budleigh Hill who 'ran on until it came to where the water crosses under the road, and they things, of course, never can abide running water, so it just couldn't get across, and off it went up in the air like a flash of fire' (Thornton 1897: 20–2). It was dangerous to have anything to do with them – paralysis might follow even an involuntary touch, and to shout at them meant death (Whistler 1908: 44; Smith 1904: 163–4). This is magical, not moral thinking. It declares that punishment will descend of its own accord on those who have, perhaps quite unwittingly, done something to break down the boundaries between this world and the other (Woods 1959: 36, 63).

In our time the dog-fiend has been gradually replaced by the dog-ghost. This development is most obvious in what are called the criterion motifs, those twists in the story which take it suddenly into a supernatural realm. At first the dog could be an household pet out for a stroll – albeit a tall, black, shaggy, bright-eyed pet. Then something brings home the realisation that this is no ordinary dog. There is a shivery sense of cold (Thelwall 1900–1). The horses pulling a carriage shy at the dog (Rudkin 1938: 118; cf. Woods 1959: 53). A real, flesh-

and-blood dog cowers and refuses to go near the strange one (Bladen 1900–1: 146; Haigh 1976; Haining 1992: 44–5). Often, the blow which is struck to ward off the dog goes straight through his shadowy form; most often, the dog vanishes or walks through a wall, bringing the sighting to an end with irrefutable proof that here was something of another world.

These are all familiar motifs; they form the stock-in-trade of the ghost story. This is the company which the Black Dog has begun to keep, and when new criterion motifs are introduced, they are taken from the same context. After all, any phantom which haunts the roads must adapt, in one way or another, with changes in traffic. When bicycles became an ordinary means of transport for rural workers, the Black Dogs who had walked beside lonely pedestrians began to pace themselves against cyclists. The need for a criterion motif was as strong as ever, so we now hear of a variant on Rhiannon's story from *Pwyll Prince of Dyfed* – the cyclist pedals like fury to get away from the dog, but however fast he goes, the dog keeps up with him (Miller 1984: 132; Linahan 1994: 35–6). Other means of transport have changed, and the stories with them. In horse-drawn days, a carriage had to come to a halt if there was a red-eyed dog lying before it in the road. But a car cannot make such a sudden stop, so instead the narrative has adopted a variation on the Bluebell Hill ghost story, the one in which the driver thinks he has run into a real girl, and stops to find that there is no-one there. It is just the same when a driver encounters a dog, like the one which vanished on colliding intangibly with a bus at Blackmoor Gate in North Devon (Farson 1978: 30)

Conventional ghost lore has influenced the Black Dog stories so much that the apparition is no longer seen as a visitor from another world, taking on the form of a dog – or of a donkey, bloodstained woman, rag of white linen etc. Instead it becomes a revenant, the ghost of a real dog which once lived nearby and which (following the rules of the modern ghost story) haunts the spot because it has been caught up in some tragic tale of loyalty and loss. At Black Dog Wood in Wiltshire, a man was killed in a fight over a girl; his dog then killed the murderer, the girl committed suicide, and now the dog haunts the scene. Or, it is a highwayman's dog that was trained to halt coaches, and did so until his master was killed by a sharpshooter, and then the dog ran wild in the woods and died shortly afterwards (Wiltshire 1973: 6). There are similar stories in Dorset (Palmer 1973: 126–7). Even Black Shuck has been given a prequel of this kind; he was the dog owned by two fishermen, or two smugglers, or a ship's captain, who were drowned in a terrible storm and washed up along the shore; and now he spends each night running restlessly between the graves (Barrett and Garrod 1976: 103–5; Westwood 2001: 111).

The change from fiend to ghost took place within a generation or so. In old Lincolnshire, one might hear how 'a huge dog-like creature, with flaming eyes, ran a mile behind a trap on a dark night, and when the farmhouse was reached, the groom fell senseless before his almost equally terrified master' (Johnson 1936–7: 83). But by the time that Rudkin came to undertake her fieldwork, the Black Dog was wondered at but not feared. Indeed, she tells one story in which his presence was welcome. 'She was returning, and noticed that a very large dog was walking behind her; this was a strange dog to her, one she had never seen before. Presently she passed some Irish labourers, and she heard them say what they would do to the lone woman if 'that (something) dog hadn't been with her'. She arrived home safely and called to her husband to come and see this fine animal, but they couldn't find it anywhere – it had completely vanished' (Rudkin 1938: 117; cf. Rudkin 1955: 390–1).

This is an instance of what one might call the 'guardian dog' tale type. These are stories in which a lonely traveller would have suffered harm from some unpleasant types, had it not been for the presence of the dog, which keeps pace with them until the danger is over and then fades away. Rudkin has another version involving a Methodist lay preacher (1938: 121–2) and this may be significant. For the earliest version of the story comes from the life of the Rev John Newton, one of the leading preachers in the generation that came after Wesley. In 1819 he was preaching the message of social conformity in Radical Manchester – a hazardous combination – and had to return home from Cheetham Hill. A dog walked beside him; two suspicious-looking men made way for the pair; and as Newton reached the city, the dog had disappeared (Jackson 1855: 98).

'Disappeared' is ambiguous, of course; did the dog vanish in a puff of smoke, or did it just wander off? There is nothing in the story to suggest that it was a phantom, but variations on the story must have spread among Methodist preachers as proof that Divine providence watched over their lonely journeys. Thomas Jackson Reynard was protected in this way, and so was another minister in Derbyshire (Mitchell 1969: 33; Daniel 1973: 44–5). By 1885 there was a retelling from Yorkshire or Durham in which the clerical status of the hero is much less important, and the guardian was definitely a phantom Black Dog (Hare

1896–1900: 5.425). In later versions, like that from Rudkin, it is a woman who is protected, and now almost any experience in which a Black Dog accompanies a woman along the road will be interpreted in this way. This tale type is only one among many stories of protection by the supernatural, and other examples of the genre have changed in the same way; the protagonist is no longer a man of the cloth, but a lonely woman (van Lieburg 2003).

Stories like this make most sense on isolated country lanes – true, there was a dog which accompanied a woman home in the small hours through the back streets of Pontefract, but she thought it was a nuisance and persuaded her husband to buy a car instead (Cunniff 1985: 29). Ironically, the padfoot of Pontefract is one of the earliest local Black Dogs on record, along with the barguest of York and the guest of Newcastle (Drake 1736: 58; Brand 1777: 74). 'Almost every town in the West Riding have their Padfoots likewise', wrote Benjamin Forster in 1766. 'Wakefield has one of its own... shagged like a Bear, as big as a calf, strange horns of an unusual form, clanking a chain from one of its hind legs, and a numerous cry of hounds behind it... Leeds has its distinct Padfoots, distinguishable one from another (as I am told) for almost every street' (Nichols 1828: 5.295–6). Until the nineteenth century, it seems, Black Dogs were a typically urban phenomenon.

Yet within a hundred years, the Black Dog had become an icon of deep countryside, walking where old traditions lingered and the street lighting was unreliable. Perhaps this was inevitable, given the changing role of rural England in the national consciousness, but filling in the details required some astute work from folklorists. Take, for instance, the marketing of Black Shuck. Throughout the nineteenth century, there were stories from East Anglia of dogs called Shuck or Shock (Forby 1830: 2.238; Gunn 1849: 307; Taylor 1850; 'T.D.P.' 1864; Gurdon 1895: 91). With the new century comes a grimmer tone; the dogs are supposed, more and more, to terrify and attack people (Kent 1910: 111; James 1891: 25–7, 32–4). A journalist, who had rashly ventured out on the coast road at Stiffkey to see if there was any truth in the old tales, was hunted down by a black shadow, and only survived by taking refuge in an isolated cottage. "Yew be a durned fool and lucky to escape at that", they said to him (Marlowe 1927: 190–204; cf. Randell 1966: 99–100; Barrett and Garrod 1976: 103–5).

Not all visitors had to learn the hard way; these traditions could be learned in advance from William Dutt's popular guide *Highways and*

Byways in East Anglia, where the dog was known memorably as Black Shuck – a name which had appeared only once before, in an antiquarian paper (Rye 1872–3: 2; Dutt 1901: 216; Dutt 1903: 331–2). As they heard the grey waves hiss on the cold Norfolk shore, every visitor to Cromer or Yarmouth wanted to know for themselves. Was it true that something elemental and savage walked here at nights? The answers came from James Wentworth Day, the aristocrat, ghost-hunter and twentieth-century impresario of Black Shuck. Actually, he hated trippers, and preferred to write nostalgically of vanished days on the Broads and Fens, where he had been on fowling trips with fellow-natives and heard their tales of the Black Dog (1954: 26–30; 1958: 201, 203–4; 1962: 640; 1967: 77, 84). They were typical local characters, these old boys; unaffected, unwashed and of uncertain temper, they lived a solitary life in the marshes, where they drank a lot and killed things, as their Viking ancestors had done before them. Wentworth Day thought that Black Shuck, too, had been handed down from the Viking past. It is not a very probable theory, but ideas about folklore are more than just theories. What was this one but a legend in its own right? – a legend of an old and savage secret, hidden somewhere deep in the country.

Every generation finds its own Grimpen Mire, that desolate place from which the baying of an enormous hound can be heard. But there is never a final explanation of the Black Dog, no Sherlock Holmes steps in to tie up all the loose ends. The end of all our studies, whether we call them folkloristic, fortean, or parapsychological, is the interpretations – the new myths, if you like – by which we hope to add something to those innumerable stories that make the mystery of the Black Dog.

A Psychological Approach to Apparitions of Black Dogs

Simon J. Sherwood

> 'The year was about 1974. I had been in bed a couple of hours. I awoke to hear a patter of feet. I looked up thinking it was my dog, but to my terror I saw a massive black animal probably with horns but perhaps ears, galloping along the landing towards my bedroom. I tried to scream but I found it impossible. The creature's eyes were bright yellow and as big as saucers. The animal got to my bedroom door and then vanished as quick as it had appeared.'

This is from a school topic book written at the age of nine or ten and describes a personal experience when I was about four years old. At the time my parents tried to reassure me by providing rational explanations. However, as this school topic book also records:

> 'I believed [my parents' explanation for my experience] until a few years later when I was reading a local paper which had an article about a haunted council house which was inhabited by a poltergeist. A variety of objects were hurled at the family's baby child. The father claimed that a black dog rushed at him and then disappeared. He also claimed that a black goat had been seen running around the house.... After reading this article I was convinced that what I thought had happened a few years back had most probably happened.'

Attempts to trace this newspaper article have been unsuccessful, although a receptionist at the local newspaper apparently recalled some details of the case and was under the impression that a clergyman from a neighbouring village was sent to this house to perform an exorcism. Unfortunately, I have not been able to verify this. As part of my quest for information about similar cases, I placed an advert in *The Psi Researcher* back in 1993 asking for information on animal apparitions, particularly black dogs. Several very helpful replies were received which revealed that black dog sightings are fairly well known throughout the UK, particularly in the Spalding area of Lincolnshire where I grew up and had my experience.

Subsequently I established that black dog apparitions have been widely reported in Great Britain, and visited Bungay and Blythburgh (see Chapters 1 and 5 of this volume). I have researched psychological and parapsychological explanations for apparitions, although apparitions of animals form only a small part of prior research. This chapter takes a psychological approach to exploring various possible explanations for black dog apparitions.

Possible explanations for apparitions

Definitions of apparitions in general vary quite considerably and some are more restrictive than others – for example, if apparitions are considered to be only animate (i.e. humans or animals) in nature – and often contain theoretical assumptions – for example, that apparitions are non-physical. S.E. Braude attempted to produce a 'theory-neutral definition of "apparition"' (Braude 1991: 191):

> *S* experiences an apparition of *x*' = df'(a) it seems to *S* as if he perceives *x* through one or more of the recognized sensory modalities, (b) *S* does not perceive *x* through any of the recognized sense modalities, (c) *S*'s apparent perception is not produced by such familiar causes as drugs, stress, suggestion, optical illusion, etc.
> (Braude 1991: 192)

Parapsychologists have attempted to classify apparitions and have proposed a number of different types: experimental[1] (where a living person attempts to make an apparition of him/herself appear elsewhere), crisis (where an apparition appears within 12 hours of the person experiencing some form of crisis), post-mortem (the apparition has been dead for at least 12 hours), ghosts/hauntings (the same apparition is seen in the same location repeatedly over time by the same or different people) (Gauld 1977; Green and McCreery

1. This is not the same as techniques designed to facilitate the appearance of apparitions before one's own self, such as the use of a psychomanteum (e.g., Moody 1994; Moody with Perry 1993; Radin and Rebman 1996; Sherwood 2000b).

1975/1989, Irwin 1999; Tyrrell 1943/1973). Many black dogs might thus be classified as ghosts or hauntings given that some are associated with a particular locality and the same (or similar) apparition might be seen repeatedly over time, often by different people. Haunting apparitions tend to show less awareness of the witnesses and may perform similar behaviour each time they appear (Irwin 1994). Approximately two-thirds of recognised apparitions are of deceased persons (Green and McCreery 1975/1989; Haraldsson 1985 1994). Such post-mortem apparitions sometimes seem to have a sense of purpose and may attempt to communicate information to the witness(es) (Gauld 1977: 603–4; Irwin 1999). Other suggested types of apparition include luminous manifestations, such as disks of light (Bayless 1973) and deathbed or take-away apparitions (Gauld 1977; Osis and Haraldsson 1986). Deathbed apparitions are known deceased persons whom a person on his or her deathbed reports have come to collect them (Gauld 1977: 606). Not all apparitions are complete; for example, certain body parts might be missing or only certain body parts might be seen (e.g., Green and McCreery 1975/1989). More than 80 percent of apparitions are of humans (Green and McCreery 1975/1989); animal apparitions are comparatively rare, and tend to be associated with domestic animals (Bayless 1973). Occasionally apparitions of inanimate objects are reported, either with or without accompanying people or animals (Green and McCreery 1975/1989).

Sometimes more than one person present will experience an apparition – such cases are referred to as collective apparitions – though not everyone present will necessarily experience the apparition (Green and McCreery 1975/1989; Haraldsson 1994; Palmer 1979; Tyrrell 1943/1973). Witnesses are usually physically inactive at the time of their experience and do not always immediately recognise that they are experiencing, or have experienced, an apparition; many do not do so until afterwards (Green and McCreery 1975/1989; Irwin 1994). A wide range of reactions are reported ranging from indifference, puzzlement and curiosity to positive emotions, such as happiness or elation, through to negative emotions, such as alarm, panic and fear (Green and McCreery 1975/1989).

Apparitions tend to appear unexpectedly and often seem very real and solid. Apparitions are usually seen in familiar surroundings, often indoors (Green and McCreery 1975/1989) and, perhaps contrary to expectations, in daylight or good artificial light (Haraldsson 1994). They may seem to be aware of their surroundings and behave as normal; for example they may leave via an actual exit, though this is not always so as some move through walls, suddenly vanish or gradually fade from sight (Green and McCreery 1975/1989; Tyrrell 1942/1963). Sometimes temperature drops are reported in the vicinity and/or the witness reports feeling cold (Green and McCreery 1975/1989; Tyrell 1942/1963). Apparitional experiences are typically brief, usually lasting less than a minute, and tend to involve only one or two sensory modalities (Green and McCreery 1975/1989); visual apparitions are the most common form (e.g. Green and McCreery 1975/1989; Haraldsson 1994; Sidgwick *et al.,* 1894), followed by auditory, such as voices and footsteps, although various combinations of sensory modalities are possible. Sometimes apparitions may touch the witnesses but the witnesses usually cannot touch the apparitions; those that succeed mostly report that their hands move straight through the apparition (Tyrell 1942/1963; Green and McCreery 1975/1989). Some apparitional experiences are restricted to a sense of a presence (Green and McCreery 1975/1989), which may or may not be identifiable. Sense of presence experiences are quite common among those who have been recently bereaved (e.g. Rees 1971; Simon-Buller, Christopherson, and Jones 1988).

So what explanations are there for black dog apparitions? Given the diversity of the features of black dog encounters, there may be more than one explanation for them. As the philosopher Braude (1991: 172) quite rightly points out, 'different sorts of apparitional phenomena may require different sorts of explanations.' We might distinguish between 'normal' versus 'paranormal' or 'supernatural' explanations for black dogs. In order to entertain a paranormal explanation one must first rule out all possible normal explanations, which can be easier said than done, so these will be considered first. Theories put forward to explain apparitions in general are applicable in this context and will be considered here (e.g., Gauld 1982; Gauld and Cornell 1979; Houran and Lange 2001; MacKenzie 1982; McCue 2002; Tyrrell 1943/1973).

Potential normal explanations

Stories of black dogs might have been made up deliberately in the past to discourage grave-robbing or to prevent children from befriending rabid dogs or entering prohibited places (see Miller 1984). Whilst being plausible for some cases, these specific reasons are not really applicable to more recent sightings. Whilst deliberate fraud is always possible, and might be difficult to rule out completely, the fact that many experients are reluctant to share their experiences suggests that most do not have attention-seeking desires that they wish to satisfy. Misinterpretation of normal experiences is another non-paranormal explanation that could involve misinterpretation of a real animal, not necessarily a dog, or some kind of misperception of the normal environment (e.g., Houran and Lange 1996), a mixture of normal and hallucinatory experience (i.e., what Green and McCreery (1975/1989) refer to as a 'metachoric experience') or an entirely hallucinatory experience. Such misinterpretation might be more likely if one has strong paranormal beliefs and/or knowledge of black dogs, particularly if one expects a particular location to be haunted.

One of the big questions is whether apparitions are objective or subjective (Braude 1991: 193; Irwin 1999: 255) but there is no conclusive answer as yet and such a question is possibly too narrow and simplistic (MacKenzie 1982: 214; Osis 1986; Price 1938–39). Perhaps apparitions are the result of complex interactions between the brain and the environment (e.g., Houran and Lange 1998; MacKenzie 1982: 208; Persinger 1989; Radin and Rebman 1996; Williams 2001). Recent research has begun to measure a range of environmental variables at allegedly haunted locations (e.g., Harte, Black, Hollinshead, and Mitchell 2001; Houran and Lange 1998; Maher 2000; Wiseman, Watt, Stevens, Greening, and O'Keeffe 2003). The following features have been proposed as support for the subjective nature of apparitions: they do not always appear to be solid; some people present might not perceive them; some apparitions can move through solid objects and sometimes people have put their hand through them; objects that appear to have moved actually have not; apparitions tend not to leave any physical traces; some apparitions may rise into the air or glide; some apparitions seem to communicate without making any sounds or using gestures (Gauld 1982; Hart 1956; Irwin 1999: 255; Tyrrell 1943/1973). The following features have been proposed as support for the objective nature of apparitions: they can appear to be solid and real; they are sometimes perceived by more than one person simultaneously; they can occlude objects and cast shadows; they can be reflected in mirrored surfaces and they can change in perspective appropriate to the witness's movement; there may be measurable or perceived changes in the environment, such as temperature changes (Gauld 1982; Hart 1956; Irwin 1999: 255; Tyrrell 1943/1973).

Archetypal imagery

The black dog might be some kind of archetypal image (see Miller 1984) shared by humans as a result of our long association and relationship with dogs in a domestic capacity. Miller (1984: 136) suggests that 'It is the depth and complexity of this special relationship that makes the dog such a potent symbol, strong enough for people to unconsciously project symbolic qualities on to real animals, or to perceive apparitions of the symbolic creature itself.' This theory is difficult to test though. Also why do only a very select few seem to have black dog experiences despite our continued association with dogs? If there is some truth to this theory then perhaps we might expect people who report black dog experiences to have a stronger link with dogs in general? Certainly this is something that could be investigated.

Cultural source and experiential source hypotheses

Another possible explanation is that one's beliefs and/or knowledge about a phenomenon might facilitate and/or somehow shape one's later experience. According to the 'cultural source hypothesis' proposed by Hufford (1982: 14; see also McClenon 1994) for supernatural experiences, 'The experiences are either fictitious products of tradition or imaginary subjective experiences shaped (or occasionally even caused) by tradition.' Even if supernatural/paranormal beliefs do not actually cause related experiences directly, there is evidence to suggest that one's beliefs (or knowledge) may shape one's experience. There is evidence from spontaneous case reports to suggest that knowledge, beliefs and expectations may influence the content of hypnagogic/ hypnopompic experiences – imagery of various sensory modalities experienced in the borderline states just as one is falling asleep (hypnagogic state) or just as one is waking from sleep (hypnopompic state) – see Leaning (1925), Mavromatis (1987), Sherwood (2002b) or Schacter (1976). For example, in one case that I have collected, an individual, who experiences hypnagogic/hypnopompic imagery and sleep paralysis ('an inability to perform voluntary movements either at sleep onset (hypnagogic or pre-dormital form) or upon awakening either during the night or in the morning (hypnopompic or post-dormital form.' (American Sleep Disorders Association 1990: 166)) quite regularly, reported that:

> After seeing Whitley Streiber's film *Communion* I did have an hallucination of one of the little blue aliens inserting [a] metal probe into my forehead.

To someone with beliefs in alien abductions, and/or a lack of knowledge about hypnagogic/hypnopompic experiences, this could have been interpreted as a real abduction attempt. I would also argue that some psychomanteum experiences, in which people report reunions with deceased relatives, involve hypnagogic/hypnopompic-like imagery and that the content of such imagery could be influenced by the beliefs and expectations of those participants too (Sherwood 2000a; see Chapter 5 2000b). Comparisons of accounts of near-death experiences (NDEs) have also found evidence of different features appearing in reports from different groups that seemed to be linked to their religious beliefs (see Greyson 2000: 321).

In my own case, the cultural source explanation seems fairly unlikely as I had not heard of the phenomenon (as far as I can remember) until years later and only very recently have I discovered that the black dog phenomenon has been frequently reported in Lincolnshire and East Anglia. However, although strong cultural traditions and knowledge of black dogs in certain areas could well influence the characteristics and interpretations of reported experiences, I am less convinced that they could cause them. Another reason why believers might report more anomalous experiences is that they might actively seek out situations in which they could have them, such as visiting a psychic or an alleged haunted house, whereas disbelievers might actively avoid such situations.

The alternative to the cultural source hypothesis, the experiential source hypothesis (Hufford 1982), predicts that certain phenomena have universal elements and will therefore occur in different cultures. If these experiences have universal characteristics, which might be deemed anomalous or supernatural, then similar experiences in different cultures should be associated with similar beliefs. The main idea is that '[s]uch experiences are instrumental in causing changes in belief, rather than merely being caused by belief.' (McClenon 1994b: 8). This hypothesis allows for people with no apparent knowledge of a phenomenon, or traditions or beliefs associated with it, to still have such experiences, whereas the cultural source hypothesis does not (Hufford 1982: 28–9). Certainly there are similarities in terms of black dog reports over time across different countries and cultures.

Much evidence in support of the experiential source hypothesis, generally, has been obtained from cross-cultural surveys of anomalous experiences and there does indeed seem to be a great deal of uniformity in the features of anomalous experience and beliefs

(McClenon 1991, 1994a, 1994b; Sheils 1978). My view is that some of the best evidence for the experiential source hypothesis comes from hypnagogic/hypnopompic experiences that have been associated with paranormal/supernatural interpretations and beliefs. Surveys have shown that such experiences often have very similar features and interpretations and have been reported in various countries, regions and cultures (Dahlitz and Parkes 1993; Firestone 1985; Hopkins, Jacobs, and Westrum 1992; Hufford 1982; Liddon 1967; Ness 1978). It is not necessarily a case of either-or when it comes to the cultural source and experiential source hypotheses though: there could be an element of both involved, although my view is that the experiential source would constitute the greater component in most cases.

In many ways, I think that hypnagogic/hypnopompic imagery plus sleep paralysis provides a fairly good and parsimonious explanation for my own black dog experience. It did occur during the night around the time of sleep; the visual image of a large black dog-like animal, seen with eyes open, was fairly bizarre and very realistic and it did move towards me in a purposeful manner. The fact that I was also temporarily unable to move or make a sound throughout my experience seems remarkably similar to sleep paralysis. Sleep paralysis is also typically accompanied by an awareness of one's surroundings and often ends suddenly and spontaneously. However, clearly not all black dog encounters occur indoors whilst the experient is lying in bed at night.

Brain-environment interaction

Another theory is that black dogs are connected with environmental phenomena, such as electromagnetic radiation, water, or 'alternative' sources of energy from ley lines (Bord and Bord 1980; Miller 1984). There has been a recent surge of interest in environmental variables in apparitional and poltergeist cases in general (see Houran and Lange 2001; Williams 2001). Persinger and Koren (2001: 179) make rather a bold claim about haunting apparitions:

> There is not a single case of haunt phenomena whose major characteristics cannot be accommodated by understanding the natural forces generated by the earth, the areas of the human brain that are stimulated by these energies, and the interpretation of these forces by normal psychological processes.

Williams provides a useful overview of evidence in support of the brain-environment interaction model of the apparitional experience but, quite rightly, notes that 'This model is only applicable to certain types of apparitional experiences, while other seemingly more complex ones remain unaccounted for.' (Williams 2001: 364). There is an implicit assumption that it is the environmental influences on the brain, in particular, and also on the body, and the interpretation of the resultant effects, which are the main causes of anomalous experiences. However, Radin (2001; Radin and Rebman 1996) has proposed more of a 'three-way feedback cycle' involving the environment, the body and the mind. In particular, Radin's theory allows for the possibility that the mind might also influence the environment as well as the reverse. His theory is based upon the results of attempts to induce apparitional experiences in the laboratory using a psychomanteum chamber, whilst investigating whether subjective and physiological changes in the participants are associated with objective changes in environmental variables. Radin's theory postulates that:

> Assuming the existence of complex interactions among mind, body and environment, we therefore suspect that at least some forms of apparitions may not be purely subjective (as in hallucinations) or purely objective (as in disembodied entities). Instead, we expect that some apparitions are – metaphorically speaking – short-term vortexes caused by short-term perturbations in a three-way equilibrium.
> (Radin 2001: 175).

Such interactionist theories are not very good at explaining the specific features of the apparitions themselves, nor collective apparitions, but are quite good at explaining the feelings and sensations associated with witnessing them. Although these theories admit to being only applicable to certain types of apparitions, they do not clearly specify which types they do or do not apply to.

The main parts of the brain believed to be involved with reports of a variety of anomalous experiences are the temporal lobes. Functions of the temporal lobes include the integration of a variety of perceptual inputs and making sense of internal and external experiences (e.g., see reviews by Persinger 1989; Neppe 1990). The main types of environmental variables measured during field investigations of apparitions and haunting include: geomagnetic fields, magnetic fields, electric fields, background ionising radiation, infrasonic waves, ambient temperature, and lighting levels (e.g., Harte, Black, Hollinshead, and Mitchell 2001; Roll and Nichols 1999 2000; Roll and Persinger 2001; Tandy 2000; Williams 2001). Other contextual variables, such as the physical appearance of a location, demand characteristics and one's personal and social beliefs can also play a role (see Lange and Houran 2001).

Research has discovered that reports of poltergeists and hauntings (Gearhart and Persinger 1986; Wilkinson and Gauld 1993), as well as sleep paralysis (Conesa 1995 1997) and epileptic seizures (Rajaram and Mitra 1981), tend to be associated with periods during which the earth's geomagnetic field has increased. The hourly incidence of epileptic seizures and some psi experiences appear to be similar too with peaks between 2 to 4 a.m. and 9 to 11 p.m. (Persinger 1989). Persinger and Koren (2001: 181) provide a list of experiences, reported by those who suffer from limbic epilepsy or complex partial seizures within the temporal lobes, that are similar to the subjective aspects of hauntings. However, a relationship between two variables does not necessarily mean that one causes the other. Nevertheless there is some experimental evidence indicating that the application of weak complex magnetic fields across the temporal and parietal lobes of the brain causes reports of a sense of presence and dancing lights (Cook and Persinger 1997). Persinger and Koren (2001: 181) point out that the threshold for the induction of anomalous experiences using such stimulation is much lower within the temporal and limbic regions of the brain. Some people also have greater temporal lobe sensitivity than others, even if they are not epileptic (Persinger and Koren 2001: 183).

A recent field investigation of Hampton Court Palace found that the average magnetic field strength was significantly higher than expected in certain areas of the 'Haunted Gallery' (Wiseman, Watt, Greening, Stevens, and O'Keeffe 2003). Other researchers have also recorded fluctuations in electromagnetic energies at allegedly haunted locations (Harte et al. 2001) though this is not always the case (e.g., Maher and Hansen 1997; Maher 2000; see also cases reported in Roll and Persinger 2001). The change in the geomagnetic/electromagnetic field strength or the level (see Roll and Persinger 2001) might be important. Changes in the electromagnetic field can be caused by artificial sources, such as power sources and machinery (Williams 2001), but also by accumulating tectonic strain (caused by changing stresses within the earth's crust) and thunderstorm activity. Persinger and Koren (2001: 180) state that:

> Areas that are prone to haunt phenomena cluster along fault lines or areas where tectonic strain accumulates. These localities are best discerned by geological maps but can be inferred by the adjacency of small creeks or rivers or indications of strain release.
> (Persinger and Koren 2001: 180)

These findings are of interest given that many black dog encounters take place near water, for example, near ponds and streams (Bord and Bord 1985: 97; Rudkin 1938). However, caution is advised: 'Lest we seem to be accepting the black dog/water link too easily, we should also note that there are very few places in Britain where one is very far away from water... ' (Bord and Bord 1985: 98). In some traditions, the black dog has been considered to be an omen of bad weather (Bord and Bord 1985: 96), and indeed allegedly appeared during a thunderstorm in Bungay and Blythburgh churches (Reeve 1988).

Electric fields might have a role to play in apparitional experiences too, at least in terms of the feelings associated with such encounters (Williams 2001). There is also some evidence to suggest that higher levels of background ionizing radiation might play a role too (Radin and Roll 1996; Williams 2001).

Infrasonic waves, generated naturally or artificially, might also account for features of some alleged apparitional experiences. For example, Tandy (2000: 360; Tandy and Lawrence 1998) discovered that a 19 Hz standing air wave can create feelings of a sense of presence and/or of being watched, a sense of fear or the perception of shadowy indescript figures, which can be misinterpreted.

Perhaps it is not a case of apparitions being either subjective or objective; perhaps they are the result of interactions between physical, neurophysiological and psychological variables and only occur when a particular combination of circumstances is present (Radin and Rebman 1996; Williams 2001). Such interactions are likely to be quite complex (Houran and Lange 1998). However, although such environmental variables might be associated with the occurrence of apparitional experiences, it is not certain whether the environmental variables cause them and, if so, how they can account for the entire specific and varying features of the apparitions. An alternative possibility is that it is the apparitions that are causing changes to the environment in which they appear.

Potential paranormal explanations

Telepathy or psychokinesis

The various telepathic theories basically suggest that apparitions are subjective hallucinations that appear to be external to the witnesses and that are created as the result of telepathic communication between the individual whose apparition is witnessed and the witness(es) (Braude 1991: 193; Gurney, Myers, and Podmore, 1886; Hart 1956; Tyrrell 1943/1973). This type of theory was originally intended only to account for living and crisis apparitions and is quite good at explaining selected features of some cases, such as veridical information being provided, the clothing worn by apparitions and the fact that some apparitions might appear as they are remembered rather than as they would have actually looked at the time (Gauld 1977: 603). The telepathy theory cannot easily account for the physical phenomena reported in some hauntings however (McCue 2002). The main difficulty with this theory is how it can explain collective apparitions witnessed by more than one person simultaneously, from each person's particular spatial perspective, and hauntings where the same deceased apparition is seen in the same location by different people over time, many of whom may not even recognise the apparition (Braude 1991 2003; Hart 1956; Tyrrell 1943/1973). Assuming that telepathy does exist, we do not yet know the limits of how it might operate so we cannot yet rule out collective telepathy (Braude 1991).

Gurney and Myers proposed the original telepathy theories. Gurney's initial theory, referred to by Braude (1991) as his 'Shotgun Theory,' suggests that each witness is independently influenced by the sender's telepathy. Gurney believed that a pre-existing rapport between those involved was required so it is difficult to see how this could apply to strangers. Gurney also suggested that infectious telepathy, where one witness influences others present, might account for collective apparitions. However, Myers criticised this latter idea and argued that if this were true then other hallucinations ought to spread via telepathic infection and this does not seem to be the case. Tyrrell (1943/1973) suggested that the apparitional drama was the result of the mingling of information from the agency of the apparition and the witness(es). Tyrrell maintained that people would only see the apparition if their physical situation rendered them relevant to the drama, e.g., if they were in the right place at the right time. Those not participating in the drama would not see the apparition and the interaction of information could explain why some witnesses' accounts might be slightly different. Both Gurney and Myers agreed that apparitions are not physical but Myers thought that they still occupy space in the 'metetherial world,' though it is unclear what he meant by this (Tyrrell 1943/1973: 45–6). Myers believed that a mental act by the sender of the apparition could cause changes in the metetherial world that would allow others to see the same hallucinatory projection. A related objectivist explanation is H. H. Price's (1939) Psychic Ether hypothesis which basically proposes that apparitions are mental images that, once created by a mind, are somehow able to persist independently in some kind of 'psychic ether' and can be picked up by others in suitable circumstances (see Braude 1991; Tyrrell 1943/1973, pp. 105-109). Johnson (see Hart 1956) expanded this Myers-Price theory and proposed that apparitions are formed as a result of sufficient chemical matter, able to reflect light, being condensed by telepathic thought-forms. How could this matter be transformed unless energy was exchanged with the environment though? Also, as Braude (1991) points out, is there any evidence that mental images can exist outside of a mind and are all images mentally created? If this were possible, why aren't there apparitions relating to people's dreams and day-dreams? It is difficult to see how this theory can account for simultaneous collective apparitions.

A related possibility is that apparitions are caused by psychokinesis (PK) (Braude 1991 2003); in other words a person's mind can cause changes in the physical environment that, in this instance, result in the creation of an apparition. Such an objectivist theory could account for collective apparitions and hauntings and associated physical phenomena, although it might require PK from the mind of a deceased individual. It should be noted that apparitions of black dogs have also been associated with reports of poltergeist phenomena (see Bord and Bord 1985: 105). Assuming PK does exist, Braude (1991: 2003) argues that, as with ESP, we do not yet understand its limits and thus cannot rule out PK as a potential explanation for apparitions at this stage. Related to the PK theory is the trace theory which, although not well-documented, suggests that events can leave a trace in a particular location that certain people might pick up on (McCue 2002). Although this might explain the repetitive, stereoptypical behaviour of some haunting apparitions how would this trace be created, in what form would it be stored and what circumstances would be required for it to be detected? If this theory is true an obvious question is why are so few locations haunted? (McCue 2002).

In the case of apparitions of black dogs, what would be the source of the telepathic imagery and/or the psychokinesis? Is it a real dog and, if so, is it living or dead? Also, if it is a living dog, what is its motivation for appearing to humans, particularly strangers, and why are the characteristics of some black dog apparitions so very different from normal dogs? The idea that black dog apparitions might be created by the mental acts of living persons has also been suggested (see Miller 1984: 136) but clearly there are difficulties with the telepathy and psychokinetic theories in this context.

Spirit hypothesis

A traditional explanation for apparitions is that they are the spirit or soul of the observed person or animal but it is difficult to apply such an explanation to apparitions of inanimate objects (Green and McCreery 1975/1989, chapter 35) and to explain why apparitions might appear to be appropriately dressed and carrying inanimate objects (Irwin 1999). The 'astral bodies' reported in some out-of-the-body (OBEs) and near-death experiences (NDEs) might be taken as support for this spirit theory (Hart 1956; Alvarado 2000; Greyson 2000). Some people believe that black dogs are apparitions of people or dogs who have suffered cruelty or violent deaths, or simply apparitions of working dogs (Miller 1984). However, how would the veridicality of such information be established (Gauld 1977) and how and why would an apparition of a dog-like creature be representing a human 'spirit'?

The spirit explanation is an objectivist theory which proposes that "an apparition is a real, localized externalized entity, and not simply a subjective construct of the percipient." (Braude 1991: 194). The fact that some apparitions seem able to adapt to their circumstances and those people present and may have a sense of motivation and purpose has been taken as evidence in support of a spirit/survival-of-bodily-death explanation (Osis 1986; Stevenson 1982). The spirit theory is more parsimonious than telepathic theories of apparitions and is better able to account for collective apparitions (Braude 1991; Stevenson 1982). The fact that some apparitions are seen repeatedly and independently by different people over time in the same location also supports the spirit theory (Braude 1991).

Supernatural

One supernatural theory of black dog apparitions is that they are real dogs possessed or controlled by the percipient (Brown 1962, cited in

Miller 1984). This theory is difficult to test and it is hard to see how this explanation could account for some of the unusual features of black dogs' appearance and behaviour in many cases. The black dog has also been associated with the Devil or believed to be a form assumed by witches and/or their familiars (Miller 1984). Such supernatural theories are difficult to test and are really beyond the scope of this chapter.

Conclusion

Although psychologists and parapsychologists have studied and investigated apparitions, their research has, perhaps understandably, concentrated upon human apparitions and there is very little mention of animal apparitions, even less so apparitions of black dogs. This is disappointing given that apparitions of black dogs are well-known in folklore, have been reported for centuries and still are being reported to this day. Although a variety of normal and paranormal explanations have been proposed to account for apparitions, some are good at explaining selected features but, as yet, none can satisfactorily explain all features nor can they accurately predict when and where they will appear, in what circumstances or to whom. Nevertheless, the psychological/parapsychological approach has a lot to offer and there is a resurgence of interest in apparitions. More attention needs to be paid to the psychology of those who report black dog experiences, the effects that such experiences can have on those concerned, and the interaction between relevant psychological, physiological and environmental variables.

Endnote

Part of this chapter is based upon an article entitled 'Apparitions of Black Dogs' that appeared in *The Paranormal Review* April 2002 and which is reproduced here with permission. I am grateful to the Society for Psychical Research for providing some funding for my research into black dog apparitions.

Infernal Watchdogs, Soul Hunters and Corpse Eaters

Alby Stone

Death and the dog

In many cultures dogs are said to be able to see ghosts and spirits or warn of impending death. For instance, in Nigeria if a dog howls outside a house early in the morning, someone in that household will die, because the dog has seen their spirit (Ojoade 1990: 219). Myths of the Kono and Mende peoples of Sierra Leone blame the dog for thwarting divine plans to make humans immortal and so dogs were responsible for the origin of death (Parrinder 1982: 56). Similar myths occur elsewhere in Africa, among the Nandi of Uganda, and in Togo, for example (Fauconnet 1968: 483, 485). Dogs are also often associated with standing vigil over the dead – the most famous example is undoubtedly Greyfriars Bobbie, the faithful terrier who kept watch at his master's grave in an Edinburgh churchyard. In ancient Iranian funerary practice dogs guarded the dead from the demon of decomposition. In many traditions spirits of the dead appear in the shape of dogs.

The phantom black dog of British and Irish folklore, which often forewarns of death, surely owes something to such a widespread belief that dogs are sensitive to spirits and the approach of death, and keep watch over the dead and dying. But the black dog is surely an expression of a more specific association of supernatural dogs (and similar animals, such as the jackal or wolf) with the journey beyond death and guardianship of the realm of the dead. In many traditions from Europe, Asia and North America such creatures are not merely harbingers of death. They are both guides to and guardians of the land of the dead. In some places dogs are also associated with funerals and the disposal of corpses. The habits of black dogs – which almost always appear at night, on lonely roads, country lanes and footpaths,

Anubis weighing the soul at the Judgement of the Dead. Funerary papyrus of Ani, 19th Dynasty.

at crossroads, stiles and gates – eerily echo ancient north-western European traditions of supernatural hounds that dwell in or about the lands of the dead. These dogs of death are reflected in myth and folklore from ancient Greece and Egypt to modern Siberia and Alaska, and find further expression in the spectral black dogs of Britain and Ireland.

Anubis

The oldest textual references to dogs or dog-like creatures in death's domain are those of ancient Egypt, which tell of Anubis, the jackal-headed deity. Anubis was patron of embalmers – and was often depicted embalming the dead – and assists at the judgement of the dead, weighing the deceased's heart against the feather of *Maat* ('Truth'). Priests officiating at funeral rites wore jackal masks to impersonate Anubis.

Anubis is sometimes shown with another jackal-headed funerary god, Wepwawet, 'Opener of Ways,' who seems to have first been a war-god before becoming a god of the dead. In their earliest forms – from the First Dynasty, before animal gods acquired human bodies – both Anubis and Wepwawet were depicted as wolves or dogs rather than jackals (Emery 1961: 123, 126–127). Another early god of the dead known from the First Dynasty period was Sed, who was depicted like the early Wepwawet, as a wolf. Other jackal-headed deities occur as minor war gods. In spite of the competition, ultimately Anubis became top dog.

From the Second Dynasty the Egyptian gods were increasingly depicted as animal-headed humans. By the time of the Middle Kingdom *Coffin Texts* Anubis was almost always shown as a man with the head of a jackal, an image that lasted into the early Christian era. However, dogs were sacred to him. Mummified dogs were sometimes placed within wooden statues of Anubis, while embalmed dogs and jackals were laid to rest in the underground cemetery at Saqqara sacred to the god (Spencer 1982: 209, 213).

As a judge of the dead Anubis is unique among otherworldly canines. In that role Anubis seems to have acquired a more general juridical aspect. There is evidence from the *Coffin Texts* that Anubis was seen as a kind of post-mortem court of appeal for legal processes that failed during a person's lifetime (Brandon 1967: 25). The Anubis tradition has a complexity not found in myths and legends of underworld dogs elsewhere in the world.

There is no doubt that Anubis was a popular and potent presence in Egyptian tradition and must have been so everywhere the Egyptians had influence. But Anubis and his fellow Egyptian dog or jackal deities were not the original canines at the threshold of death, except insofar as their archaic forms resemble the underworld hounds of less sophisticated traditions. They may be counted part of the same continuum. The distribution of such dog traditions across the Northern Hemisphere clearly signals that the dog was imagined as an underworld guardian or guide long before the establishment of Egyptian culture.

The Indo-European hellhound

The Greek hellhound Kerberos (Cerberus in Latin), the watchdog of Hades, famously charmed to tameness by Orpheus, drugged by Aeneas and wrestled into submission by Herakles, is probably the best known of the dogs of death. According to Hesiod's *Theogony*, Kerberos was one of two monstrous dogs fathered by Typhon upon the half-serpent nymph Echidna:

> First, Orthos the dog of Geryon, and next,
> Unspeakable Cerberus, who eats raw flesh,
> The bronze-voiced hound of Hades, shameless, strong,
> With fifty heads.
> (Wender 1973: 33)

Kerberos is depicted with a single head on a Corinthian cup of about 580 BCE; and only ever has two heads on Attic vase paintings (Carpenter 1991: 130). But he is more familiar as a three-headed hound[1]. He is clearly a counterpart of the two dogs of Yama, king of the dead, who guard the path to the next world in Indian myth (*Rig Veda* 10.14.11. In ancient Iran two dogs protect the Cinvat ('separation') bridge that leads from this world to the next (*Vendidad* 13.9). Other examples are found in Armenia and pagan Scandinavia. Reconstruction of the Proto-Indo-European myth indicates that these were originally thought of as a dog of life and a dog of death. One carried off those about to die while the other could restore life. Death's watchdogs are generally described as dark or speckled: Armenian legend names them Spitak ('the White') and Siaw ('the Black'). The Indo-European hellhound is a 'black dog of death' (Lincoln 1991b: 97).

Ancient Iranian funeral ceremonies were inextricably linked to the dog. To ward off the demon of decomposition required a rite known as the *sag-did*, the 'dog's glance' – this was supposed to be performed by a 'four-eyed' dog, or a white dog with yellow ears. As such dogs have always been something of a rarity, this was usually interpreted as a dog with a spot over each eye – though in practice, any dog would do. These represented the dogs that protected the Cinvat bridge, the Iranian hellhounds (Darmesteter 1887: lxxxvi–ii).

Dogs were important to the myth and religion of the Celtic peoples. The animals are depicted as the companions of various deities on Romano-Celtic religious sculptures in Britain and Gaul, and were often sacrificed or sometimes eaten at ritual feasts. The rich iconography of the Gundestrup cauldron – found deposited in a Danish bog, it is usually associated with Celtic religion, although it was probably of Thracian manufacture – includes a dog underneath a cauldron in which a man or child is being immersed head-first in what is usually considered to be a sacrificial act. In the Roman period many dogs were deposited in pits and wells, which Miranda Green believes points to a strong connection between dogs and the underworld. Some dog

1. The heads of Kerberos vary in number, from one or two on the vase paintings to three in (for example) Sophocles' *Women of Trachis* and fifty in Hesiod. It seems probable that the two-headed Kerberos represents a Greek rendering of the two dogs of Indo-European proto-myth. The three heads may have come about through Kerberos' later association with Hekate. The fifty-headed version appears to be a conflation of the dog of death with groups of fifty (warriors or hounds) found elsewhere in Greek tradition, such as the hounds of Actaeon. The original pair in Greek tradition was probably Orthos (who is also two-headed) with Kerberos – the two are sometimes shown as a pair. Orthos is spoken of in dual form in Pindar's first *Isthmian Ode*.

Two-headed Kerberos with Herakles, Athena, Hades and Persephone. Attic black-figure amphora from Cervetri, c. 520 BCE.

deposits are clearly sacrifices to chthonic powers. For instance, at the Romano-British town of Caerwent, tribal capital of the Silures, five dog skulls were placed in a well near a circular shrine. Numerous dogs were deposited in a deep well associated with a first century shrine at Muntham Court in Sussex. The remains of sixteen dogs, together with a complete Samian bowl, were placed in a second-century well at Staines near London. Seven pups and an adult bitch were buried in urns at Upchurch Marshes in Kent. Green observes that dogs 'seem to have a particular association with sacred sites which have an aquatic connection' (Green 1992: 111).

Other Celtic dog burials fit well with literary traditions of dogs as otherworld guardians or psychopomps. A row of dogs' teeth, perhaps a magical protective device, was found 'set as though in a necklace' in

Three-headed Kerberos. Laconian cup, c. 560 BCE.

Detail of the
Gundestrup cauldron.

the ditch of a ritual site with a sacred pond at Ivy Chimneys (Witham, Essex). Similar burials and ritual deposits are found on the Continent, where there is also evidence for dogs buried to accompany humans to the Celtic afterlife (Green 1992: 111–13). A dog skeleton was recently discovered buried at the entrance to an Iron Age ritual complex on a hilltop in south Leicestershire (Priest, Clay and Hill 2003; Bob Trubshaw, pers. comm.).

Ritual dog burials predate the Iron Age in Britain. A clear example from British archaeology of the dog's function as a guardian to the spirit world is the two dogs found with an impressive alignment of wooden posts at the Flag Fen complex near Peterborough, in use in the Neolithic and Bronze Age. The dogs appear to have been ritually killed to serve as spirit-guardians, at a site that was evidently a major focus for funerals and other rituals over many centuries. At Caldicot in Gwent another Bronze Age site provides evidence for a dog buried in a manner which strongly suggests it was intended as a ritual guardian. (Green 1992: 111).

The Indo-European hellhound did not pass from view following the triumph of Christianity. On the contrary, Cerberus was adopted by Christian writers and given a prominent place in Hell, probably thanks to the popularity of Virgil's *Aeneid*. For instance, Cerberus ('Cerbere') is the gatekeeper of Hell in the fifteenth-century mystery play *Passion d'Arras*, in which he also narrates the Crucifixion, and in Arnoul Gréban's *Mystère de la Passion*. In the hands of Christian writers, Cerberus was transformed. In the twelfth-century *Roman d'Eneas*, an anonymous adaptation of Virgil's epic into French,

> ... his legs and feet are shaggy, with hooked toes and claws like those of a griffon; his back is sharp and bent, with a hump on the spine, while from his narrow shoulders hang massive arms with hands like hooks; on his three sinuous necks are manes of serpents, and three dog-like heads complete the hideous picture. No longer is he a monstrous dog, but rather a dog-like demon with arms and hands instead of legs and paws... we see a stage in the process of degeneration of figures from Classical myth that took place in the Middle Ages. In the case of Cerberus, this process was to continue until he was able to figure on the stage as one of the principal devils in the mystery plays.
> (Owen 1970: 143)

The underworld guard dog also survived in recent Celtic folklore. A Gaelic tale collected on the island of Barra in 1859 tells of a fairy woman who would come each day to borrow a cauldron from a herdsman and his wife on Sandray, returning it with flesh and bones still in it as payment. One day when the wife was away the fairy woman came as usual but the husband became afraid and forgot to say the words his wife usually spoke, which bound the fairy to returning the vessel filled with food, and it was not returned. The wife went to the fairy mound to fetch her cauldron, but found only an old man at home. As she took her pot, the old man set two dogs on her ('Loose the Black, and slip the Fierce'). However, she stopped the dogs by upending the pot so that they stopped to eat the meat and bones it held (Westwood 1985: 515–16).

The Germanic hellhound

The Indo-European hellhound also survived until relatively recently in northern Europe. In the medieval Icelandic poem *Baldrs draumar* the god Baldr has bad dreams, so Óðinn rides down to Niflhel on his eight-legged horse Sleipnir to find out their meaning.

Up rose Óðinn, the ancient god of sacrifice,
and on Sleipnir laid the saddle.
Downward he rode to Niflhel;
he met a hound that came from Hel.

It was bloody about the breast,
and at the Father of Spells
he howled long. Forward rode Óðinn,
the earthen path thundered,
at last he came to the house of Hel.

Another encounter with underworld guardian canines occurs in the thirteenth-century *Gesta Danorum* of Saxo Grammaticus (8.240). Saxo tells of a Danish expedition led by King Gormo and guided by one Thorkillus. After crossing a river spanned by a golden bridge, 'a natural boundary between the human and the supernatural worlds,' the Danes arrive at a place that is surely a realm of death:

> ... a gloomy, decayed town, looking most of all like a misty cloud. Stakes raised at intervals along the battlements displayed the severed heads of men. Before the gates [the Danes] saw dogs of uncommon savagery keeping vigilant watch over the entrance.
> (Saxo Grammaticus 1979: 264–5)

In another Norse poem, *Fjölsvinnsmál* (part of a longer poem, *Svipdagsmál*), we learn of two hounds who keep ceaseless watch – one sleeps by day and the other by night – at the otherworldly hall Lyfjaberg in Jötunheimr. Svipdagr asks the watchman Fjölsviðr (in other poems this name belongs to Óðinn) what they are called. He is told

One is called Gífr,
and the other Geri,
if you want to know that;
very ancient guardians
and they keep guard
until the gods are torn apart.

The hall, surrounded by a wall of flame, is the abode of Menglöð, whose name ('Necklace-Glad') may identify her as the goddess Freyja. But although she is described as a sun-bright maiden there is good reason to believe that here Menglöð is the underworld goddess Hel under another name, and Lyfjaberg is a realm of the dead.[2] The dog

Geri shares its name with one of Óðinn's wolves – the other wolf is called Freki – with whom the god shares that other well-known abode of the dead, Valhalla.

Garmr is another dog often mentioned in connection with Óðinn. According to *Grímnismál* (44), Garmr is 'the best' of dogs. In *Völuspá* (43, 48, 57)

> Garmr howls mightily before Gnípahellir
> Breaks his chains and runs loose.

According to Smorri Sturluson's *Gylfaginning* (51), when Garmr breaks loose at Ragnarökr and the gods confront demons and monsters, he and the god Týr will destroy each other.

Garmr is an enigmatic creature. Rudolf Simek (1993: 100) thinks there are 'no grounds' for identifying Garmr with the bloody hound of *Baldrs draumar*, but suggests he might actually be the wolf Fenrisúlfr, 'a case further supported by the dog's fetters'. Turville-Petre (1964: 281) agrees. However, Simek also observes that the *Gylfaginning* snippet about Garmr and Týr is probably Snorri's work rather than an authentic tradition. This means that the chain is the only thing that argues for Garmr having been the same as Fenrisúlfr prior to Snorri's rationalisation of Norse myth. It is just as plausible that Garmr is a chained watchdog. Furthermore, Garmr howls outside Gnípahellir, 'cave of the steep (or 'overhanging') mountain,' or perhaps 'peak of Hel' (Lincoln 1991b: 104), a name that suggests nothing less than an

2. In some ways *Svipdagsmál* resembles the *Sleeping Beauty* story, but it has a distinctly sinister feel. Svipdagr is given an impossible task – to find and wed Menglöð – by his stepmother. From the beginning, it is clear that Svipdagr is doomed to succeed. He starts by consulting his dead mother in her burial mound. From that and his subsequent conversation with Fjölsviðr we learn that there is absolutely no way into Lyfjaberg – except for someone called Svipdagr, who is welcomed in as soon as he reveals his identity. There is none of the heroic action or magic we might expect from such a tale – indeed, the poem seems to drip with macabre irony. Although it suggests a link with Freyja, Menglöð's name might equally be a reference to death by hanging or strangling. This idea is supported by the name given to a clay wall surrounding the hall – Gastropnir, 'Guest Strangler'. Ellis (1943: ch. 7) has convincingly identified Menglöð with the goddess Hel, on the grounds that there are enough significant parallels between Niflheimr and Lyfjaberg to suggest that the rulers of the two places were also probably meant to be one and the same.

Alskog Stone.

entrance to the underworld. When the underworld guardian leaves his post nothing can prevent anyone getting into – or out of – the land of the dead. The image of Garmr unchained smacks of the Christian Day of Judgement, a theme that has clearly influenced *Völuspá*. Although Simek (1993: 114) remarks that it is 'pure speculation that Gnípahellir is situated at the entrance to Hel,' there seems little reason to suppose otherwise.

In the tenth-century Scandinavian poems *Eiríksmál* and *Hákonarmál* dead kings are described as entering the hall of Óðinn after their last battles. When they arrive at Valhalla they are welcomed by valkyries, one of who greets them with a horn of ale. Similar scenes are depicted on stone sculptures from Gotland: one, from Alskog, appears to show a stylised hall resembling a burial mound and a dog which 'could be the dog mentioned in mythological poems as guarding the road to the land of the dead' (Davidson 1993: 33).

The Old English epic poem *Beowulf* describes the monster Grendel and his mother in terms that leave little doubt as to their lupine nature. Among the words used to describe them are *werga, werhðo, heorowearh, brimwylf, grundwyrgenne,* all of which contain elements denoting the wolf (*wearg/wearh* and *wylf*). Grendel and his mother are haunters and guardians of a burial mound in marshland. This brings to mind the bodies of water – usually rivers, but sometimes a lake or sea – that typically have to be crossed to reach the Indo-European underworld, and those of some non-Indo-European cultures.

Grendel is also called a *scucca* ('demon'), from which the second element of the name of Black Shuck, the supernatural dog encountered by nocturnal travellers in East Anglian folklore, is derived. It is also said of Grendel that, 'from his eyes shone a fire-like, baleful light' (*him of eagum stod ligge gelicost leoht unfæger*) (Newton 1993: 6).

The underworld dog may be traced back quite a long way in Germanic tradition. It is associated with the goddess Nehalennia, whose name occurs on numerous votive remains dating from the second and third centuries in the Netherlands and the north-west of Germany, along the Rhine from its mouth as far as Cologne.

Nehalennia's name has been subjected to several etymological studies, of which two in particular stand out. One sees the middle element *-hal-* as the most significant and links it to the Germanic names Hel, Holda, Holle and so on, and Greek Kalypso, which come ultimately from Proto-Indo-European **Kolyo* 'the one who conceals', a chthonic death-goddess associated with hanging or strangulation (Lincoln 1991b: 78). The other interpretation prefers to connect the first element *neh-* with the Latin verb *necare* 'to kill' and Greek *nekus* 'corpse', which leads toward much the same thing, a goddess of the dead (Simek 1993: 229). Objects associated with Nehalennia frequently show the goddess enthroned, with cornucopias, loaves and baskets of fruit or grain on her lap, and frequently with a dog by her side. She is sometimes shown with one hand on a ship, or an oar. The foodstuffs have swayed various writers, who see Nehalennia as a goddess of fertility and prosperity, but bearing in mind the frequent appearance of ships in Germanic funerary contexts, the remaining

Nehalennia and her dog. Stone relief from Colijnsplaat, Netherlands.

iconography – including the dog – and her name suggest a mortuary role.

Death's watchdog in Eurasian and North American myth

The hound that guards the gate of hell is not confined to Indo-European tradition. Finnish tradition also has an infernal watchdog. Louhi, the Mistress of Pohjola (the land of the dead), lives on a cold, gloomy island of a river at the edge of the world, guarded by a fiery dog. The dog's role is defined in a Karelian variant of the *Song of Vipunen*:

> ... the mistress of Pohjola
> Bid her serving maid go see,
> What the watchdog was barking at,
> Why the island's dog was frantic:
> No watchdog barks for nothing,
> Nor should the island's dog be frantic.
> (Siikala 2002: 161)

In the *Kalevala* (12) Lemminkäinen employs a demon to 'block the barker's mouth' so that he can slip unnoticed into Louhi's house. When he is noticed the Mistress of Pohjola sarcastically remarks:

> There used to be a dog here
> A cur iron-hued
> That ate the flesh, gnawed the bones
> Lapped the blood of someone new.
> (Bosley 1989: 143)

This dog is also known as a traditional helper (though it can also be an adversary) of the *tietäjä*, the cunning man of modern Finnish folklore, relic of a vanished Finnish shamanism. *Tietäjä* songs name it 'Blacky, the black dog, cur with iron fur':

> I had a black dog long ago
> A cur the colour of iron,
> Its mouth a hundred fathoms wide,
> Its jaws as broad as six axe-handles...
> (Siikala 2002: 107)

The supernatural beast is also known as the Dog of Pohjo (i.e. 'the North'), the dog of Tuoni, or the Hound of Manala, or the 'Dog of Lappland, iron-toothed, the runner of the eternal shore' (Siikala 2002: 107, 119, 235). Tuonela and Manala are other names for the Finnish underworld, which was believed to lie in the far north or in Lappland. Rota, a Saami god of the dead, is also a master of hounds (Pettersson 1957:159).

Death's watchdog is a widespread theme in other circumpolar traditions. The Chukchi of eastern Siberia believe that the dead must pass through the 'country of dogs' to reach the otherworld (Bogoras 1904: 143). When a Yukaghir shaman follows the road to the underworld he finds a house where an old woman lives, with a barking dog outside (Jochelson 1924: 205). Dogs guard the entrance to the Koryak underworld (Jochelson 1904: 103). In Altaic shamanism fierce dogs guard the subterranean *yurt* of Erlik Khan, king of the dead (Eliade 1964: 202).

In North America, the underworld watchdog is widely distributed. In Greenland Inuit myth, Arnagnaksak the queen of the dead is guarded by dogs (Pettersson 1957:167). In another Inuit tradition a dog with bared teeth guards the entrance to the undersea home of the goddess

Takánakapsâluk (Eliade 1964: 295). The last is not strictly a mortuary realm but it has clear parallels to lands of the dead in other traditions. Ojibway myth has 'the dog with the bloody mouth that devours the souls of those who have tormented dogs' standing guard on the underworld road – a post-mortem punishment also found in, for example, Menomini and Shawnee belief (Hultkrantz 1957: 80), and which occurs in Siberia among the Chukchi and Koryak.

Guide dogs to the other side

The vast Indian epic *Mahabharata* (17.3) tells how Yudhisthira, king of the Pandavas, sets off on a tortuous journey to the Hindu sacred mountain Meru with his five brothers, their joint wife and a dog. One by one, Yudhishthira's companions die of exhaustion but he survives and 'enters heaven in his mortal body, not having tasted death'. The devoted dog survives too, but when it enters heaven with him the gods are horrified. It is then revealed to be Dharma (the cosmic order) in disguise. In another story Dharma inhabits a cremation-ground in the guise of a hideous, black-skinned man wearing funeral garlands, holding a skull and thigh bone, and surrounded by a pack of dogs. Although these and other features mark the incarnate Dharma as an outcast his appearance also has the ring of a death-god about it. Moreover, when the long-suffering Hariscandra – an Indian equivalent of Job – goes to work for Dharma at the cremation-ground he has a bad dream in which he visits first hell then heaven (White 1991: 84–5).

Another seeker of heaven is conducted to a paradisal realm by a dog in the tenth-century *Navagatio Sancti Brendani* – better known as the *Voyage of St Brendan.* The very first island the saint and his crew of monks come to is a rocky island with steep cliffs. The monks eventually find a landing site and disembark.

> Then a dog appeared there, approaching from a small path... the brethren followed the dog until they came to a large mansion, in which they found a spacious hall laid out with couches and seats and water for washing their feet.
> (Gardner 1989: 87)

This is a typical Irish otherworld: a rich and hospitable hall on an island. As the isle is Brendan's first landfall after leaving Ireland, and the first of many otherworldly islands he visits, it is fitting – if ironic – that the clerics should be led to its fine hostel by a canine guide straight out of pagan tradition.

The late twelfth-century *De Nugis Curialium* of Walter Map tells of a little man who turned up at the wedding of Herla, an ancient British king, riding a goat. Herla agreed to attend the diminutive stranger's wedding in a year's time. When the day came, the little man led Herla to a cave and they came at last to a palace illuminated by many lamps. When the wedding was over, Herla and his retinue were laden with gifts, including a small bloodhound that had to be carried. They were told not to dismount until the dog jumped down. When they emerged they found that centuries had passed and when some of Herla's men dismounted they turned to dust. The king warned the rest not to dismount before the dog left his arms. The story continues: 'The dog has not yet alighted' (Westwood 1985: 307). Since then Herla's company has often been seen in its ceaseless wandering.

Herla's story has something in common with the Wild Hunt. However, the dog is clearly associated with the boundary between the fairy world and this one. Unusually, it is not simply a guide to and from the spirit world – rather, it keeps Herla and his people alive in liminal timelessness until they leave its sphere of protection, a perverse gift that brings immortality but allows the recipient no peace.

There is some evidence that in Anglo-Saxon England dogs were occasionally sacrificed to accompany dead humans to the afterlife. At Illington (Norfolk) a child was buried with a dog, the only animal remains found at the site (Owen 1981: 87). A woman was buried with a small dog at Minster Lovell (Oxfordshire), while men and dogs were buried together at Foulden (Norfolk), Mitcham (Surrey), Cookham (Berkshire) and in two graves at Loveden Hill (Lincolnshire). There are indications that some of these dogs were pets, as we would understand the term today, while a few elderly beasts may have been retired hunting dogs. All seem to have been killed to accompany their deceased owners into the next world (Wilson 1992: 100–1).

Turning to Finland, a dog appears to act as a psychopomp in an episode from the *Kalevala* (36), in which the hero Kullervo returns home after a long absence and seduces his sister, who afterward drowns herself. The distraught Kullervo goes off to war but returns home to find that all his family have died. As he weeps over his mother's grave, he hears her voice:

> 'Well, I've left Blackie the dog
> so that you can go hunting:
> take your dog with you
> go hunting yonder

> up into the wilds...'
> Kullervo, Kalervo's son
> took his dog with him
> trudged off up the road
> up into the wilds
> and he went a little way
> stepped a tiny bit of road
> and he came to that islet
> he happened upon the place
> where he had ravished the wench...
> (Bosley 1989: 494)

When he comes to the place where he made love to his sister Kullervo is overcome with despair and throws himself upon his own sword. The dog's presence in this episode seems quite irrelevant, a trivial detail, until we think of the black dog of the Finnish underworld, and the mother's advice takes on a grim tone.

The Kullervo story should perhaps be seen in the context of the practice of killing dogs as funerary companions in the customs of other Uralic-speaking peoples and their neighbours in Siberia. For instance, at Evenk funerals a reindeer and a dog are sacrificed – the deer is eaten but its bones, together with the dead dog, are bound to a tree or post (Czaplicka 1914: 155). The Golds sacrifice a dog by the graveside (Baldick 2000: 142).

The psychopomp dog has also become embedded in Christian tradition. The Eastern Orthodox churches usually depict St Christopher as a dog-headed giant. This image was used as early as the fifth century in a Coptic text telling of Reprobos, a cynocephalic savage renamed Christian upon his conversion – clearly an early version of Christopher. In later legend, Christopher was said to be a member of a race of dog-headed eaters of human flesh who could only communicate by barking. Christopher was first given the gift of speech by an angel to demonstrate the power of God, then was converted to Christianity when he carried the infant Christ across a river. Christopher was originally black but his skin became white when he was baptised.

David Gordon White (1991: 35) notes that the saint is rarely portrayed as dog-headed in Western Christianity. However, two Old English sources describe him in canine terms. According to the Old English *Passion of St Christopher, se wæs healf hundisces mancynnes*, 'he was of the race of mankind who are half hound'. The Old English *Martyrology* elaborates upon this: he was 'from the nation where men have the head of a dog' (*of þære þeode þær men habbaþ hunda heafod*) and 'from the country where men devour each other' (*of þære eorðan on þære æton men hi selfe*). Furthermore, Christopher had 'the head of a hound' (*hundes heafod*) and very long hair. His eyes 'shone as bright as the morning star' (*his eagan scinon swa leohte swa morgensteorra*), and 'his teeth were as sharp as a boar's tusks' (*his teð wæron swa scearpe swa eofores texas*) (Newton 1993: 5–6).

Plainly this is not quite the patron saint of travellers that we are told about at Sunday School. In the context of Western Christianity it is a peculiarly Old English view of St Christopher. With his shining eyes and aquatic associations he resembles the lupine monsters of *Beowulf* rather than the popular image of a saint. Furthermore, like most other Indo-European traditions, the Germans seem to have conceived of an otherworldly ferryman who conducted the dead to the underworld. Indeed, Óðinn appears as a sinister ferryman in some medieval Norse texts, such as *Völsunga saga*. It seems reasonable to suppose that St Christopher's appearance and occupation struck a traditional chord familiar to English ears, and that the legend was consequently coloured further by Germanic underworld motifs.

However, Christopher is not the only saint associated with cynocephaly. The dog-headed Coptic saint Mercurius, who was obviously derived from the Roman psychopomp Mercury, had two dog-headed attendants. In German folklore St Thomas is also believed to appear as a dog or a dog-headed man – though he acts more as a soul-hunting hound of the Wild Hunt than a guardian or guide (White 1991: 37–8, 40).

The guide dog to hell was also known in early modern London. Newgate Gaol was the scene of a haunting by 'a walking spirt in the likenesse of a blacke dog, gliding up and down the streets a little before the time of Execution.' Luke Hutton, a criminal executed at York in the late 1590s, left behind an account of the phantom hound. Published as a pamphlet in 1612, *The Discovery of a London Monster, called the black dog of Newgate* suggested the dog was the ghost of a scholar imprisoned in Newgate who had been killed and eaten by starving inmates. One view is that the phantom was invented by gaolers as an additional torment for prisoners, for whom cannabalism was occasionally a necessary evil (Ackroyd 2000: 248). But a slightly later (1638) account tells of a spectral black dog that rode beside condemned criminals in the cart that took them from Newgate to the gallows (Simpson and Roud 2000: 25) suggesting that Hutton's black dog may have evolved from, or later merged with, the old idea of a canine psychopomp.

The Wild Hunt

Irish and Welsh vernacular literature and folklore hint strongly at a close connection between hunting and the chthonic otherworld. In the *Mabinogion* story *Pwyll Pendevic Dyvet,* Arawn, king of the underworld, has a pack of white, red-eared dogs, whose colouring proclaims their otherworld origins. According to the early Welsh 'Taliesin' poem *Cwn Annwn* ('The Hounds of the Underworld') the eponymous dogs were death omens, described as small, speckled and greyish-red, chained and led by a black, horned figure. These ghostly dogs appeared only at night to foretell death, sent from Annwn to seek out corpses and dead human souls.

The Cwn Annwn are clearly forerunners of the Wild Hunt, the spectral, demon-led pack that haunts Britain and parts of Europe, especially Germany, under a variety of names. In Cornwall the hounds are known as Dando's dogs or the Devil's dandy-dogs, either the pack of a sinful priest named Dando or the hounds of Satan himself. On Dartmoor they are the Wish (or Wisht) Hounds; or the Yeth Hounds or Yell Hounds – 'heath' or 'hell' hounds, in the local dialect. In the north of England the Gabriel Hounds – also known as Gabble or Gabriel Ratchets – are usually identified with nocturnal sounds made by birds, especially geese. These phantom packs are usually an omen of death or disaster, and are often said to be either damned souls or demons hunting the souls of the dead. The *Peterborough Chronicle* for 1127 reports a ghostly hunt with hounds 'all black and wide-eyed and loathsome' that appeared when the rather unpleasant Henry of Poitou was appointed abbot at Peterborough Abbey (Westwood 1985: 187).

A Robin Hood tale associated with both Fountain Dale (Nottinghamshire) and Fountains Abbey (Yorkshire) provides an intriguing combination of the Wild Hunt with the St Christopher legend. There are several different versions of the ballad known as *Robin Hood and the Curtal Friar.* All agree that Tuck and Robin take turns to carry each other across a moat to and from an island, and that on the way back Robin dumps the Friar into the water. In one version Robin blows his horn and calls up his men. Tuck does likewise to summon his dogs, and a truce is called. A later version has a fight in which the dogs catch Robin's comrades' arrows in their mouths, though some hounds are killed (Knight 1994: 61–3). Here we have the typical underworld theme of crossing a body of water, with the guardian hound expanded to form a pack. One variant of the tale has fifty hounds, which echoes the fifty heads attributed to Kerberos (Trubshaw 1994b).

There is some overlap too between the underworld guardian hound and the Wild Hunt. Adam of Bremen tells how a group of Frisians sails to an island in a cold, dark region. This seems to be a land of the dead – it is similar to the land of lifeless shades encountered by Gormo and Thorkillus in a *Gesta Danorum* episode that immediately follows the one discussed above. When the Frisians start carrying off the treasure they find there, they are chased off by gigantic men with huge hounds that kill one of their number (Ellis 1943: 187–8).

Martin Puhvel observes that in Germany 'crossroads are probably the commonest gathering-place' of the Wild Hunt, 'not surprisingly in view of their notoriety as ghost-infested places.' However, he notes that in Germany and the Netherlands crossroads were also believed to be a place of refuge from the spectral hunt, as they were an obstacle to the hunters – an idea found in connection with the Cwn Annwn (Puhvel 1989 105–12). This seeming contradiction seems to derive from the crossroads' liminal nature. Crossroads – sacred to Hekate, a death-goddess with a canine aspect who was closely associated with Kerberos – are places between places. As with other interstitial sites, the dead and their abode are close by. We also have the idea that the choice of direction offered by such a junction can confuse spirits and demons.

The dog's dinner

In the funeral practices of various peoples dogs are more than just companions or guides through the afterlife. In nature the dog is a scavenger and carrion-eater, and this trait has been usefully employed by humans to dispose of the dead, by giving corpses to dogs to eat. For instance, in Siberia, the custom at Kamchadal funerals is for the dead to be left a short way from the door of their *yurt* to be eaten by dogs, which the deceased would have power over in the next life (Czaplicka 1914: 145).

Dogs are also employed to devour the dead symbolically. Among the Finnic-speaking peoples of the Volga food sacrificed to the dead is given to dogs, which are thought to be in contact with the departed (Pettersson 1957: 110). At Gilyak funerals the tables are turned – dogs are sacrificed in honour of the dead and thrown on the funeral pyre, but mourners eat parts of the animals (Czaplicka 1914: 152).

Whenever humans ritually become the dog's dinner, the rationale is that the dog will carry the deceased to the next world or be a servant to the dead. In this way the corpse-devouring dog is also a psychopomp. This may also be one reason why the jackal Anubis is portrayed as an embalmer – one who prepares a corpse for death. We see here another correlation with the Wild Hunt, and with the fearsome Kerberos.

Lincoln (1991b: 98–9) points out that the names Grendel, Kerberos, Garmr, Geri and Gífr are all related. *Gífr* means 'greedy' in Old Norse, as does *Geri*. The latter is also the name of one of Óðinn's two wolves in *Gylfaginning* and *Grímnismál*. Bruce Lincoln has shown that these names are all derived from the same Proto-Indo-European root, **gher-*, which is thought to denote the sound made by an animal, in this case the canine variety. In essence, the names are onomatopoeic and all mean 'growler'. The same source gives rise in Greek to *Kerberos*. Lincoln also points out that the root has given rise to a class of words that he describes as 'sub-verbal utterances: sounds commonly made by people, none of which constitute actual words'. He concludes that the Indo-European words so derived refer to greed as 'that characteristic whereby a human being is reduced to the level of a hungry beast: growling, ravenous, and inarticulate'. Lincoln also suggests that the dog's association with the underworld is due in part to the dog's widespread reputation as a devourer of corpses, hence the curse 'dogs shall gnaw you in Hel' which is uttered in the Norse sagas. The growl of the hellhound denotes 'the greed of none other than all-devouring death' (Lincoln 1991b: 100).

The nature of the beast

But the humble dog has a noble aspect too. People have employed dogs as guards and hunters for many thousands of years. Wherever there are humans there are dogs, usually loved and prized for their devotion, courage and tenacity. And those dogs go about their canine business in death as they do in life. In the native traditions of Eurasian and North America the land of the dead is much like the land of the living. The dead do much the same as they did when they were alive (Stone 2003: 112). The same seems to have been true for early Indo-European traditions (Stone 1998: 124–6). For instance, in Finnish lore the Mistress of Pohjola lives in a village that is pretty much like any ordinary Finnish village, apart from its unnatural gloom. Her dog behaves like any other watchdog, barking at intruders. The same is true of hunting. The hounds of hell may have become specialised as hunters of the dead, loosed at night to bring the deceased to their new, post-mortem home, but they are still doing what dogs have been kept for down the ages.

But dogs are dangerous creatures. For all their tameness and ease in human company, dogs are still animals. They inhabit a halfway state between the domestic and the feral. Watchdogs are tame and docile with their own humans but aggressive and wild toward strangers. Hunting dogs live with people but typically are in packs, just as they would be in the wild. The dogs of death appear at crossroads, at gates, on roads and bridges. Kerberos and his fellow underworld watchdogs are, like their mortal counterparts, always at the threshold, neither fully in the home nor wholly out of it. That is why St Christopher and other canine entities are effective psychopomps – the dog's existence in the in-between, liminal places allows it access to other worlds and to sense the inhabitants of those realms. The central characteristic of the hellhound is its intermediary position at the border of this world and next, between life and death. The dog is perfectly suited to this role – it is the quintessential domestic animal, the tamed carnivore that stands midway between beast and human, the wild and the civilised.

The cynocephalic St Christopher embodies this idea: half-human and half-canine, he belongs to both worlds and to neither. He straddles places, always in transit. The same could be said of jackal-headed Anubis and Wepwawet, openers of ways. The dog-aspected Dharma belongs to no caste and can take a person to heaven or to hell. But as dog-men they – like the hounds of the Wild Hunt – are akin to the corpse-eating dogs that, by absorbing the dead, can take them to the mortuary realms.

> In the last analysis, the hellhound is the moment of death, the great crossing over, the ultimate turning point.
> (Lincoln 1991b: 101)

Friend or Foe?

Norfolk Traditions of Shuck

Jennifer Westwood

> ... young children fly terror-stricken along the roads at night fearful of meeting Shuck...
> *(Harper's Magazine* October 1893)

In 1946, I used to cycle to and from the school bus stop alone, along a narrow lane through woods near my south Norfolk village. I was six years old. I had heard of the Shuck Dog, probably from other children, and still remember the fear at night, where the woods crowded close to the road, full of rustlings and scufflings, or when the wind was blowing hard and I was unable to hear if he was coming pad-pad-pad down the road behind me.

This exploration of the bogey of my childhood begins with three narratives:

> Mr E. Ramsey, of Bawburgh... recalls as a young man, cycling home late one moonlit night from a darts match in Norwich. As he was approaching the village he saw - 'the biggest hound, sitting by the signpost, that I had ever seen ... Its eyes shone like coals of fire ... Half a mile further, I heard him, coming up behind, his paws beating the grit road. `My God, he's coming for me.' Instead, he passed me, so close I could smell his rankness.

> The hound ... suddenly stopped on the fringe of the spinney, in the middle of the road, facing me. To me, he looked aggressive [sic]. So I stopped, with my cycle between me and the hedge, hoping someone would come along to help me. Just then there was the roar of a vehicle, coming through the

> spinney. It came through with no lights, and was careering from side to side. The great hound was right in its path, as it hit it.
>
> The vehicle came so close that I fell into the hedge with my cycle on top of me.... Picking myself up, thinking the hound had come to a bad end, I was amazed to see it still standing there.... I ... felt fear in my heart, of knowing what the hound would do, if he came for me. To my surprise he turned, and was gone. Neither left nor right, just vanished.
>
> They do say that anyone seeing him, is the sign of death, to one's self or next of kin. All I can say is, on that night he saved my life...
> (Reeve 1988: 67–8)

Mr Ramsey wrote to me in 1995, when nearly eighty, saying that, 'I remember well that night and, at the time, I did not think of this hound as old "Shuck", the devil dog.'

In about 1986, the late Ann Todd, the film actress, wrote to me:

> I have a cottage near the sea at the village of Walberswick in Suffolk and a few years ago was sitting on the beach with my dog – a very physic [sic] Sealyham, when he suddenly jumped up growling and then ran around in circles barking & wagging his tail, as if playing a game (the hairs on his back standing up) and I saw a large black dog floating round him, 2 feet off the sand – they seemed to be enjoying themselves and when the phantom dog faded out, my terrier searched and searched for him. On the way home I stopped at the sweet shop in the village and told the old lady who runs it what I had seen. She answered 'Ah, that was Chuff – he died in ... (I can't remember the date) how many chocolate balls did you say you wanted Miss Todd?

In 1991, Mrs Nancy Raby Lawson sent this account relating to Bacton on the north-east coast of Norfolk:

> As children, spending the summer hols at Bacton, we were always welcomed by the group of fishermen who operated their crab boats from Rudrum's Gap. After 70 odd years I have always remembered the story told by Mr Woodhouse (dead many years ago), of the two fishermen, Grimes and

> Rudrum, who jointly owned a large black dog who always went in the boat with them on fishing trips. One night they were all drowned. One body was washed up and buried at Happisburgh, and the other washed up and buried at Overstrand, and their dog, also drowned, was said to spend the night running along the cliff from one grave to the other. A faithful friend, rather different from the legendary 'Black Shuck'.

There is obviously some distance between the bogey of my childhood and the dog-guardian, playful dog-phantom and 'faithful friend' of these three narratives. We might dismiss them as idiosyncratic, were it not that kindly-disposed phantom dogs are known from other areas. Theo Brown (1979: 79) wrote of the entity known generically as 'The Black Dog': 'Where dogs are denigrated, the ghost is held to be evil; where they are held to be noble, the spooks are good and even protective.' One might add that perceptions of these dogs may have changed with time, as a side-effect of the changing attitudes to domestic animals generally (Thomas 1984: 100–9).

For *pace* Mrs Lawson, the 'faithful friend' is certainly a form of Shuck. Overstrand bore a black dog on its village sign, in commemoration of Shuck's oldest recorded 'run'. The Quaker tract writer, Mrs Amelia Opie, heard about this run when staying at Northrepps Cottage in January 1829, and later recalled the local belief that 'at twilight every evening, the ghost of a dog is seen to pass under the wall of Overstrand Churchyard, having started from Beeston...' (Hooper 1894). The ghost-dog's 'beat' ran from Beeston towards what is now Cromer railway station, and from there followed a route along the coast to Overstrand which, in the 1920s, though it had been built over, locals still knew as 'Shuck's Lane.' The 'beat' of the 'faithful friend' *south* from Overstrand looks suspiciously like a rival run.

That the 'faithful friend' is Shuck is confirmed in newspaper correspondence from the 1960s (Loveday: 4): '"Shuck" travels between Blakeney, Sheringham and Overstrand and is supposed to be searching for his master who was shipwrecked on the coast.' Another contributor sends a poem telling the same story, but involving two smugglers, Will and Ben, and 'their old dog Shuck.' Both are essentially the same tale as one told by Barrett (1976: 105) of a ship's captain and his wolf-hound drowned in a ship-wreck.

The stereotype of Shuck

The apparition known as Shuck is a kind of hallmark of East Anglian folklore. Much has been written about him, generally based on a handful of sources. He appears in many guidebooks as a firm article of belief, but features in few local legends which are not late or literary. Writers on Shuck from the mid-nineteenth century to today have reduced and summarised the material, degrading variety into stereotype. A more standard image of him is purveyed than ever existed. Enid Porter (1974: 89) wrote: 'Portent of death and disaster was Black Shuck, the calf-sized dog that haunted – some say still haunts – Norfolk and Suffolk' and ascribed to him the motif numbers E.423.1.1.1(b) (Ghostly black dog); E.421.3.6 (Ghosts as dogs with glowing tongues and eyes); and E 574 (i) (Ghost of animal as death omen). This over-simplifies.

The basis for the stereotype was laid down in the early nineteenth century. The Reverend John Gunn, rector of Irstead, in the Broads, set out to record 'the traditions... retained in the memory of a single individual.' That individual was Mrs Lubbock, an uneducated washerwoman then in her eighties, but intelligent, with a highly retentive memory. Much of what she knew had been learned from her father, so reaches back into the eighteenth century.

Unfortunately, when publishing his results, Gunn embedded her testimony among details gleaned elsewhere, in order 'to show that my venerable washerwoman is by no means solitary in her opinions.' He writes:

> The ordinary form which spirits are said to assume in East Norfolk, is that of the Phantom-Dog, stated by Mrs Lubbock to be a headless dog, with saucer eyes, who is said to pass nightly over Coltishall Bridge; while another, 'Old Shuck' by name, travels between Beeston and Overstrand, the terror of the neighbourhood. A lane in the latter parish is called after him, 'Shuck's Lane'
> (Gunn 1849: 307)

The punctuation of this passage suggests that all we can rely on Mrs Lubbock having said was that the phantom dog was 'a headless dog, with saucer eyes.' However, we also learn that, to Gunn's mind, there was more than one dog, that one bore the name of Shuck, and that phantom dogs had their regular 'beats.'

stern one, nor shalt thou old shock *[ne schaltu aide schuke]* moot with me no more. But fly sorrowful thing out of mine eyesight... (Cockayne 1866*:* 65–8)

However, while the derivation from OE *scucca is* attractive, the variants of the name 'Shuck' suggest a richer semantic history than perhaps has been allowed. Relative to Magdalen's Shucky Dog are the adjectives *shucky* and *shacky,* defined by Forby (1830: 294, 299) as 'shabby, ragged' and 'shiftless or shirtless'; and *shack,* both verb and noun, meaning respectively 'to rove about' and 'shabby fellow, lurking and prowling about...' (Forby 1830: 294). Both shabbiness and prowling could be considered attributes of Shuck. A connection might be made with *shag,* 'a rough dog' (Johnson 1827: *3), shucky* being also, from at least 1850, Norfolk dialect for 'shaggy' *(Notes and Queries* 1850: 468). This would relate the apparition to the Shag-foal and Buckland Shag, of other counties, and to 'Monsieur Shagg,' the supernatural Black Dog of Newgate, described in a pamphlet of 1638 as a 'walking spirit' with 'two sawcer-like eyes, and Iron chaine about his necke' *(Discovery of a London Monster* 1638: 1–2).

In a list of dogs in *Macbeth,* Shakespeare includes 'shoughs' and 'water-rugs.' Dr Johnson glossed *shoughs* in this passage as 'what we now call shocks.' The word *shough is* cited in the *OED* (2nd ed.) from 1599 and refers to a kind of lap-dog. It may find a late echo in Chuff of Walberswick, whilst the 'water-rug' reminds one of Lyng's Old Rugman.

Under *shock,* attested from 1638, the *OED* gives: 'A dog having long shaggy hair, *spec.* a poodle'; it also cites *shock-dog,* from 1638 onwards. Formally, this is the equivalent of Norfolk 'Shuck Dog.' Are Shuck and Shock two separate entities, with separate names and separate etymologies? Or did *shough, shock* and *shock dog* share with Shuck a derivation from OE *scucca*? How do we fit into this the fact that hair standing on end from fright – horripilation – is symptomatic of the presence of the supernatural? As Charles Kent (1910: 111) notes: 'It is a terrible feeling... this being tracked by Shuck, and generally ends in ... giving way to fright, when... the hair stands erect on the head, the vocal chords refuse their work, and then ensues a swift panic-stricken flight with Shuck grimly following... '. A shock-head is still someone whose hair stands on end, as from an electric shock, and there is an old pink known to gardeners as White Shock, round-headed, densely double and toothed – the Shock-headed Peter effect.

Characterisation

Colour

Can it be coincidence that 'in northern Europe at least a sixth of all dog-demons are black poodles' (Dale-Green 1966: 54) or that Boy, the white standard poodle killed in battle at Marston Moor, was accused in a series of Parliamentarian pamphlets of being Prince Rupert's familiar? (anon. 1642; anon. 1643; anon. 1644)

Boy brings us to a consideration of Shuck's appearance in detail. He is often black, as are Magdalen's Shucky Dog and the Hateful Thing of Geldeston, in the Waveney Valley (Adams c.1914: 187). That he was formerly *invariably* black cannot be assumed, however: his appearance and behaviour relate him to the normally white phantoms Galley Trot of Woodbridge (Moor 1823: 142) and the fiery-eyed White Rabbit of Thetford (Clark 1926: 171), as well as 'a great white dog, like a grey-hound' that started running alongside two men who were crossing the marshes of Flegg. Only one of them could see it, and he suddenly swore and said: 'That come right up beside me and licked my hand.' He 'died within the twelvemonth' (Loveday: 5).

Coat

Shuck's coat is normally 'shaggy' (*Notes and Queries* 1850: 468; Rye 1872–3: 2–4; Hooper 1894; Kent 1910: 111; MacGregor 1955: 66).

Head and eyes

Earlier sources emphasise his huge, saucer eyes which he retains even when headless (Gunn 1849: 307; Hooper 1894). Although educated collectors found this 'somewhat anomalous' (*Notes and Queries* 5, 1864: 236), it is doubtful whether their informants meant the description to be taken literally: headlessness and saucer eyes are both traditional recognition signs of the supernatural.

Old Scarf, Skeff of Garvestone and the Hethersett Faines are distinguished by these great eyes, reminiscent of the eyes of the supernatural dogs in Hans Andersen's *Tinder Box*. Eye-colour is often mentioned: Rye's Shuck Dog and Black Shuck have 'great yellow eyes,' and Old Shuck has eyes 'like a couple of lamps in a yellow postchaise' (Rye 1877–87: 293; 1897: 62). This was updated to eyes 'like railway lamps' in Jimmy Farman's description of the phantom he encountered in the marshes near St Olave's in about 1939 (Haining 1992: 44–5). In other accounts, the phantom is said to have 'fiery eyes,' and Rye (1872–3: 2) heard that, around Salhouse, Black Shuck was a Cyclops, 'with a blazing eye in the middle of its forehead.'

Invisible or shadowy

According to Porter (1974: 89), Shuck is sometimes invisible. The Hateful Thing is visible only to some. More often the phantom is only dimly perceived. Charles Kent, speaking for Methwold, on the edge of the fens, before the First World War, says: 'No one has really seen his whole shape, for he does not come near enough to reveal himself...generally remaining in shadow' (Kent 1910: 111).

Silent or padding

Shuck is also said to 'pad along noiselessly', 'his footfalls make no sound', 'a noiseless phantom... ' (Rye 1872–3: 2; Dutt 1901: 216; *Norfolk and Norwich Notes and Queries,* 3rd series, 1, 1906: 105). At the beginning of the twentieth century, however, the Methwold Shuck advertised his presence by sound: 'the pit-a-pat of his feet are distinctly heard' (Kent 1910: 111), and though Adams maintains that the paws of the Geldeston Hateful Thing make 'no sound upon the ground,' his only eye-witness, a carter's wife, contradicts this:

> It was between eight and nine ... when we met Mrs S., and she started to walk with us, when I heard something behind us, like the sound of a dog running. I... paid little attention to it, but it kept on just at the back of us, pit-pat, pit-pat, pit-pat!
>
> 'I wonder what that `ere dog wants,' I said to Mrs S.
>
> 'What dog do you mean?' said she, looking all round.
>
> 'Why, can't you hear it?' I said. 'It has been following us for the last five minutes or more! You can hear it, can't you, Josh?' said I.
>
> 'Nonsense, old mawther,' said Josh; 'jest you lug hold of my arm and come along.'
>
> I was walking between Josh and Mrs S., and I lay hold of Mrs S.'s arm, and she says:—
>
> 'I can hear it now; it's in front of us; look, there it be!' And sure enough just in front of us was what looked like a big black dog; but it wasn't a dog at all; it was the 'Hateful Thing'... (Adams c.1914: 187)

Mr Ramsey too heard the phantom coming up behind, 'his paws beating the grit road' (see above). Other noises natural to a dog are heard: an eyewitness reports that 'something panting came from behind' and a great black dog as big as a calf followed her and her father for a quarter of a mile, its tongue hanging out 'like a great piece of red flannel' (Day 1962: 639). Only among the fishing community at Lower Sheringham in the 1860s, where he was a presage of storm (T.D.P. 1864: 236), was Shock a noisy elemental, like Jan Tregeagle in Cornwall, or the Spectral Herdsman of the Norfolk salt marshes who, 'when the rolling mists came in from the sea ... would be abroad, driving the helpless cattle before him, with weird cries...' (*Norfolk and Norwich Notes and Queries,* 3rd series, 1, 1906: 106)

Shuck as death omen

The ominous nature of Shuck is habitually mentioned by both writers and informants. Rye says: 'To meet him means death to the meeter in the course of the year...' (Rye 1872–3: 2), a belief supported by a 'witness legend' of a farmer who, on seeing Shuck, drove his cart straight at him and touched him, and within a short time died (Hooper 1894). However, it is not borne out in practice: 'sightings' of Shuck commonly come from long-term survivors. His appearance as a portent of someone *else's* death, especially that of a close relative, is still frequently mentioned, for example by a correspondent who reports seeing a phantom dog near Walberswick in July 1986, and having local friends identify him as Shuck and connect him with the death of her father in the same month. At Lowestoft in the 1970s, Shuck's appearance was claimed to have presaged the loss of a fishing vessel with all its crew (Reeve 1988: 67). More rarely other disasters, such as the burning down of a cottage, are reported, or anticipated; at Geldeston, the Hateful Thing's appearance presaged a future 'act of horror' on the site.

The idea that Shuck is a portent of death may be a tradition more honoured in the breach than the observance: out of seventy-four 'sightings' compiled from eyewitnesses in 1977, only seventeen could be connected with death or even misfortune (Reeve 1988: 42). A man who had seen Shuck many times indeed told Wentworth Day (1962: 640) that 'it didn't do no harm.'

The terror by night

If Shuck's role as an omen is exaggerated in the printed record, often underplayed is his character as a terror. Chuff of Walberswick raised no alarm in the living dog's breast, but this contrasts sharply with the experience of Jimmy Farman:

> He crossed my path down by the dyke and my old bitch almost went mad with fear. Crouched down she did, and the hairs rose up on her back as though they were bristle. For some minutes I couldn't get her to move; no, not a step; and she moaned terribly, just like a child.
> (Haining 1992: 44–5)

Meetings with Shuck also terrify horses. From 1900 comes an encounter in an unspecified location:

> The grandfather of this present chronicler was driving home one evening from holding an inquest in Marshland.... He noticed the mare trembling very much as though with fear, and ordered the groom to dismount from the gig and see what ailed her, when ... a waft of cold dank air struck both men as in the light of the lamps a large black dog of supernatural size passed over the road from ditch to ditch in front of the trembling little mare, which could scarcely be pacified.
> (Thelwall 1900: 297)

Human beings too are normally petrified by Shuck. Speaking of his childhood in Magdalen, Cambridgeshire, Arthur Randell, born 1901, writes of how his father would come in at night saying that the Shucky Dogs were about (Randell 1966: 99–100): 'Then the doors would be locked and all the lights put out.' He goes on to tell a story about an old man evidently frightened to death by a Shucky Dog, for there he was in his cottage dead, with a terrible expression on his face, and in the snow outside were a dog's paw prints, leading to his door but not away.

The fear of Shuck is not wholly a supernatural one. Animals can evidently expect physical attack. Old Scarf was known to maim horses and cattle, and Shuck was certainly disposed to maul human beings. Forby (1830: 238) says of Old Shock: 'Those who are so foolhardy as to encounter him, are sure to be at least thrown down and severely bruised, and it is well if they do not get their ancles sprained or broken; of which instances are recorded and believed.' The Melton Shock left its tooth-marks on a man's thumb to his dying day (Gurdon 1893: 91–2); Old Scarf threw a man over the hedge (*Norfolk and Norwich Notes and Queries*, 1, 1906: 105); a boy's neck was 'fearfully lacerated' by

Shuck at 'a small seaside hamlet' somewhere along the East Anglian coast between Felixstowe and Hunstanton (Adams c.1914: 128); a man who met him near Stiffkey was 'found in the morning with his throat torn' (Marlowe 1927: 190). Running away made things worse: Galley Trot 'gives chase to those whose alarm compels them to run' (Moor 1823: 142); whilst the person who sees the Hateful Thing should not attempt to turn back or he will snarl and growl like a mad dog. 'He has been known to drag children along the road by their clothes, and dire disaster overtakes the individual who persists in running away from him' (Adams c.1914: 187). By contrast with this record of violence, Mr Ramsey's ghostly saviour (see above) is not unparalleled: a black dog acted as guardian and guide to women rush-gatherers out late at night at Catfield c.1842 (Loveday: 15), much as black dogs escorted women in the lonely lanes of Lincolnshire.

Explanations of Shuck

Like similar phantoms elsewhere, Shuck is occasionally accounted for, by implication, as the revenant of a person: the Melton Shock haunted a spot where a man had fallen from a wagon and broken his neck (Gurdon 1895: 91–2); and Thelwall (1901: 297) says: 'Childhood's traditions always connected a gallows with these spectral dogs.'

Shuck and Shock are connected with churchyards by Mrs Opie (Hooper 1894) and Taylor (1850: 468), while the Geldeston Hateful Thing, also called the 'Churchyard Beast,' haunted the glebe. The eyewitness mentioned above watched him go 'right through the wall' into the churchyard and vanish (Adams c.1914: 192). These churchyard dogs are possibly vestigial Church Grims, but the guarding of a churchyard is never explicitly stated. In the accounts of Mrs Lawson and Ann Todd (see above), phantom dogs are explained as the revenants of dogs. Similarly the black dog frequently sighted near Barnby this century is said to be the ghost of a dog decapitated on the railway line (Loveday: 19). Shuck is also sometimes explained as a hoax or practical joke: a pony or ram tricked out by smugglers to scare away the inquisitive, a large ram with a lantern tied to its head and a long chain dragging and clanking after it, which a farmer dressed up to frighten his friends (Rye 1872–3: 2) or a 'poor dickey' got up as a demon to cause general alarm (Hooper, 1894). If these explanations are not simply rationalisations, they certainly exploit pre-existing traditions.

Shuck as Devil

Accounts of Shuck leave no doubt as to his diabolic character. The Hateful Thing, locally regarded as a 'swounding' (something that made one swoon), was also called the 'Hell-hound' or 'Hell-beast' and specifically said to be of diabolical origin (Adams c.1914: 188). Scorch marks and the smell of sulphur, both traditionally associated with diabolic visitation, are mentioned in 'sightings' (see above). Hooper (1894) writes: 'Only the other day I was told of a man driving towards Rockland with a companion, when suddenly right in their path stood a huge uncanny dog. The driver pushed on... but as the cart touched the Thing the air was alive with waving flame, and a hideous sulphurous stench loaded the atmosphere.'

Another diabolic feature is the heavy chain which the phantom sometimes drags behind him (Randell 1966: 100; Hooper 1894). The novelist Sir Henry Rider Haggard, who farmed at Ditchingham, where a phantom dog was to be seen, remarks: 'Indeed, once I met him myself at this very spot [Hollow Hill], looking saucer-eyed in the twilight and clanking an appropriate chain...' (Rider Haggard 1899: 26). An eyewitness in (probably) the 1960s records that '... one night very late I was cycling from Sheringham when, to my surprise, `Shuck' was running beside me with his chain clinking on the ground' (Loveday: 5). Another eyewitness, who in 1968 encountered the black dog often seen near Barnby, also reported a rattling chain (Loveday: 19). This chain is a sign not only of a dog broken loose from its kennel (as it turned out in Rider Haggard's case) but, from at least Elizabethan times, a ghost returning from imprisonment in Hell.

We are told of Old Scarf that, if a straw were placed in his path, he would rattle his chain and howl (Hooper 1894). Left unexplained by Norfolk antiquaries, this is illuminated by Northumbrian legend:

> Beyond Farne are the Noxes, and E. and W. the Wide-opens, islets connected by a submarine chain of rounded stones, where St Cuthbert heard the fiends shriek as they played in the spray before the storms, and the monks drew a fence of straw signed with the holy cross along the sands between them and a demon pack of goatriders...
> (Walcott 1861: 375).

These aspects of Shuck conform well with Elizabethan and later ghost-lore, and seventeenth-century ideas of Black Dogs as manifestations of the Devil. The dog as the Devil lingers in a story said by its recorder to be told along the East Anglian coast by the 'beach-folk' (Adams c.1914: 126–8). This notion also dominates Black Dog traditions in Scandinavia. However, though Shuck is still referred to in print as a 'demon dog,' probably no one today literally believes that he is a diabolic apparition.

Shuck as Black Dog

The Reverend Gunn wrote: 'The ordinary form which spirits are said to assume in east Norfolk, is that of the Phantom-Dog.' Shuck is almost invariably a black dog in both folkloric accounts and reported 'sightings' today. But in some ways he is not characteristic of the species. Theo Brown (1979: 79–80) mentions as a curious fact 'that we do not appear to have any record of a Black Dog requiring conjuration ... no one seems to have suggested exorcizing them.' Whatever may be true of the West Country, this is not so in East Anglia. A black dog was formally conjured at Blickling according to a (possibly literary) story preserved by Augustus Hare (1896–1900: 6.303–4), and we are told of Old Scarf at Yarmouth that 'eventually the clergy took him in hand ... and with solemn rites chained him in the cellar of the Duke's Head. Candles were thrown over the bridge into the water and `Scarf' was doomed never to reappear until the candles were burnt out, i.e. until St Tib's Eve' (Hooper 1894), in other words never.

Theo Brown (1958: 176–8) draws a distinction between true Black Dogs, appearing in that form and no other, and having particular beats or runs, and a range of shape-shifting bogeys, with odd local names, which only sometimes took the form of a black dog. She groups Shuck along with such shape-shifters as the Barguest and Padfoot. Though Shuck does have the particular runs mentioned above – Shuck's Lane, Overstrand, Lovers' Lane, Geldeston, Coltishall Bridge – and also Market Hole (Day 1958: 203–4), he is not confined to them and he certainly has shape-shifting in his background. Shock appeared in Suffolk mainly as a dog, sometimes as a calf, but also sometimes with 'a donkey's head and a smooth, velvet hide' (Gurdon 1895: 91–2).

Adams' account of the Hateful Thing implies that only sometimes did it appear as a dog and indeed he describes 'the wraith of a donkey, which... rattles chains and breathes forth fire' haunting the glebe between Lovers' Lane and Geldeston church, the Hateful Thing's own 'beat' (Adams c.1914: 187, 195).

In Suffolk, Galley Trot 'sometimes assumes the shape of a dog... is sometimes as big as a bullock... not very definable as to outline' (Moor 1823: 142). Yarmouth's Old Scarf also appeared as a huge black goat (Brown 1958: 178); the donkey-headed Melton Shock which, in the 1860s, 'hung on the toll-bar gate' (Gurdon 1895: 91–2) sounds something like the Cambridgeshire Shug Monkey (Day 1954: 28).

The Black Dog of Bungay

Even the celebrated Black Dog of Bungay can be a shape-shifter. As recently as the 1970s, an old lady born in Bungay said that the Black Dog was actually a black cat who entered the church and attacked the congregation. She had sung this rhyme about it in her schooldays:

> Scratch cat of Bungay,
> Hanging on the door,
> Take a stick and knock it down,
> And it won't come anymore.
> (Reeve 1988: 71)

This 'scratch cat' notwithstanding, the Black Dog of Bungay has doubtless reinforced local ideas of Shuck as a black dog. Its history can be found elsewhere. Essentially, the second edition of Holinshed's *Chronicles* reports that in 1577 a terrible storm hit Bungay and Blythburgh, during the course of which what may have been ball lightning entered the church in each place, killing several people. One of the editors of Holinshed was the Puritan divine, Abraham Fleming, who retold these events in a tract entitled 'A straunge and terrible Wunder' as the visitation of a great black dog. This was a natural thing to do. People in the sixteenth and seventeenth centuries interpreted tempests, whirlwinds and related phenomena as the work of the Devil, just as they had during the Middle Ages, when the demons of tempest might appear in churches in animal form (Dale-Green 1966: 53–4). Fleming's was consequently not the only pamphlet of the period reporting animal-demons assailing churches during storms (Westwood 1985: 148). In East Anglia, the notional connection between electrical discharge and the supernatural was preserved in speech into the nineteenth century, when Forby (1830: 319) defines the word 'spirit' as 'electric fire; a blast of lightning,' giving as an example: 'In the great tempest, a spirit lit upon the church steeple' (cf. Moor 1823: 382).

It would be difficult to prove that traditions of the Black Dog of Bungay have been in continuous oral circulation since the seventeenth

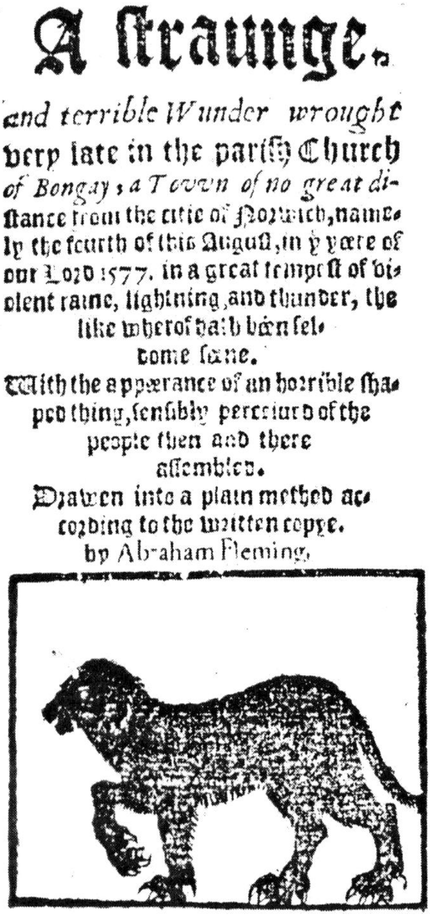
A straunge.
and terrible Wunder wrought
very late in the parish Church
of Bongay, a Towne of no great di-
stance from the citie of Norwich, name-
ly the fourth of this August, in ye yeere of
our Lord 1577. in a great tempest of vi-
olent raine, lightning, and thunder, the
like wherof hath been sel-
dome seene.
With the appearance of an horrible sha-
ped thing, sensibly perceived of the
people then and there
assembled.
Drawen into a plain method ac-
cording to the written copye.
by Abraham Fleming.

The title page of A Straunge Wunder in Bongay *describing the black dog seen in Bungay, Suffolk, 1577. Reproduced by kind permission of Fortean Picture Library.*

century. More likely, interest was rekindled when a new edition of Fleming's pamphlet was published in London in 1826, which included a versified account of events and a lurid illustration. In the 1930s people were again reminded of the Black Dog in local publications, notably Ethel Mann's *Old Bungay* (1934). Today the Black Dog is the official symbol of civic identity: Bungay's coat of arms, granted in 1953, shows him standing on a forked lightning flash; he appears as a weather-vane near the Butter Cross and the town football team is known as the Bungay Black Dogs.

There is no truth in the claim made by some writers that the marks of the Black Dog's claws, said by Fleming to have been left on the church door at Bungay, can still be seen. Little remains of the sixteenth-

The north door, Blythburgh church., with marks said to have been made by the black dog. Photograph by Simon Sherwood.

century original, destroyed in 1688 in the Great Fire of Bungay (Reeve 1988: 2, n.1 and 72). However, at Blythburgh, when the north door (traditionally the Devil's Door) was cleaned in the 1930s, long black marks were found which are confidently shown to children as the marks of the Black Dog's claws. With such visible reminders to reinforce it, the story is still developing. For example, the Black Dog is now sometimes said to be the ghost of Hugh Bigod, first Earl of Norfolk, haunting Bungay Castle (Coxe 1973: 105; Hurren 1994).

Whether or not the Black Dog and Shuck are identical is still debated in books, but apparently not by locals. Reported encounters with the Black Dog in or around Bungay are not distinguished from encounters with Shuck elsewhere. In one account, the apparitions are positively identified (MacGregor 1955: 67). When Shuck is identified in this way, he loses his shape-shifting character and appears only as a black dog.

Shuck as *Hound of the Baskervilles* and hound of Odin

Out of this identification as a black dog, new ideas are emerging. It has entered regional wisdom that Shuck inspired Conan Doyle with his fake phantom in *Hound of the Baskervilles* (1902).

Black dog weathervane, town centre, Bungay, Suffolk. Reproduced by kind permission of Janet and Colin Bord / Fortean Picture Library.

Peter Haining sets out the argument in *The Supernatural Coast* (1992: Ch.3) but this is contradicted by Sir Arthur Conan Doyle's own preface to the story (1981: 668). Film versions from 1909 on may well have helped shift the physical image of Shuck away from the 'shock-dog' towards the hound.

I was taken aback one day in 1995 when the curator of a Norfolk museum, speaking to me about Shuck, pronounced his name 'Shewk'. It occurs to me now that he had taken seriously what I believe is a myth in the making. In 1994, Angela Hurren wrote in the *Eastern Daily Press*:

> Shuck is thought to be the oldest phantom in Britain, his legend coming to the country with the Viking invaders and their legends of Odin's black hounds and Thor's own dog, Shukr.

As with the Black Dog of Bungay in the 1930s, this seems to be a more or less conscious manipulation of the tradition by regional writers, in this case springing partly from a desire to find a context for local beliefs in a larger pattern of pagan antiquity (East Anglia's answer to the Celtic revival), partly to use mythology as a flag of regional identity.

I do not know where 'Shukr' springs from, but we can trace the Scandinavian connection at least as far back as Walter Rye, who quotes a 'friend' as saying that Shuck was a 'Scandinavian fiend' (Rye 1872–3: 2). One influence was the Manx Mauthe Doog (Mothey Dhoo), made famous by Sir Walter Scott who featured him in *Peveril of the Peak* under the name Mauthe Dog. Actually Sir Walter probably mistook Dhoo (Gaelic *dhu* 'black') for dog – the Mothey Dhoo was a shape-shifter.

Nevertheless, people began to refer to black dogs everywhere as the Mauthe Dog. Rev G. Munford, in *Local Names in Norfolk* (Munford 1870), suggested that Mautby derived its name from the Mauthe Dog, and possibly this encouraged Rye to insert in his glossary of East Anglian words (Rye 1895: 138): '*Mawthe-dog. The phantom of a dog in Norfolk [Pr.Pa. (Shuck? W.R.)].' We might be forgiven for thinking that "Pr.Pa.", the *Promptorium Parvulorum*, provides some basis for the form. However, it contains neither 'mawthe' nor 'mauthe', nor any related word.

What attracted both Munford and Rye to the Mawthe-dog was that the Isle of Man, its home, was formerly a Norse kingdom. Though their notion of an East Anglian Mauthe Dog of genuine Viking extraction is wishful thinking, the idea was accepted without much question. Likewise M. Knights (1889: 64) links them all by implication, mentioning the Moddhey Dhoo and then continuing: 'A similar legend was, till a comparatively late period, connected with deep and narrow lanes in parts of Norfolk, where the folk were of Scandinavian descent.'

By the mid-nineteenth century, British antiquarians had compared the northern Gabriel Hounds 'with Odin's Hounds – Odens hundar, of Swedish folk-lore, the hounds, black... and fire-eyed, which always accompany the infernal hunt... ' (*Gentleman's Magazine* 1866 part 2: 189). The shift from pack to solitary dog may have been accomplished as far as East Anglian tradition is concerned in 1872 by Charles Hardwick. Speaking of the Wild Hunt, he relays a German tradition of a hound 'sometimes left behind in the household, through which the wild hunt has passed' (Hardwick 1872: 171–2). He comments: 'I am inclined to think that the "Trash" or "Skriker"... has some relationship to the strayed hound of Odin... ' (Hardwick 1872: 173).

Trash was a shape-shifter appearing most often as a large shaggy dog with eyes as big as saucers. Once a connection had been made between the 'strayed hound of Odin' and Trash, it simply jumped like a spark to another traditionally saucer-eyed, shaggy dog, Shuck. Whether or not the first to make the connection, the *East Anglian*

Handbook for 1885 says of Shuck that 'Mr Hardwick supposed him to have some connection with the strayed hound of Odin' (p75). On the fertile imagination of East Anglian nationalism, it passed from hand to hand, each writer apparently assuming that there was some mythological validity behind the label (see Hooper 1894; Dutt 1901: 216), down to James Wentworth Day, who in 1954 wrote of Black Dogs generally: 'All have their roots in the Hound of Odin, the mighty dog of war, whose legend came to Britain a thousand years ago when the long-ships grounded in the surf, [and] the ravens flew at their mastheads... .' (Day 1954: 30) The hounds of Odin have now been disseminated by mass-market publishing (Readers' Digest 1977: 29).

As for 'Thor's own dog Shukr', I do not know that Thor had a dog, and doubt he would have called him Shukr. Whoever started this hare running, I shall watch the course with interest. I had thought from my reading of Keith Thomas (1973) that the reason for the concentrations of black dogs in Scandinavia, Germany and Great Britain that Rye and others point to has less to do with ethnic origins than with the Reformation – that with medieval precedent helped by the theory of familiars, one of the forms the Devil took was commonly a supernatural black dog.

Shuck and the Norfolk Black Puma

Where now? Today the Norfolk Black Puma, reported from 1993 onwards, is often mentioned in the same bated breath as Shuck. I am sometimes asked if I think that they are one and the same, and the answer is yes, in a way I do. For all the cages we try to put him in, Shuck remains protean, unpredictable, wild, a survivor.

A shorter version of this chapter was previously published in H.E. Davidson and A. Chaudhri, (eds), *Supernatural Enemies* (Carolina Academic Press 2001) and reproduced by kind permission.

See also Mike Burgess's Web site devoted to phantom black dogs in Norfolk, Suffolk and Essex (www.shuckland.co.uk/), which went online after this chapter had been written.

Black Dogs in the New World

Bob Trubshaw

I got to keep movin'
I've got to keep movin'
Blues fallin' down like hail
Blues fallin' down like hail
Umm mmm mmm mmm
Blues fallin' down like hail
Blues fallin' down like hail
And the days keeps on worryin' me
There's a hellhound on my trail
Hellhound on my trail
Hellhound on my trail.

So sang the blues singer Robert Johnson in 1936–7. Johnson's biography is blurred by mystery and myth-making; in conformance with a well-established legend, he was alleged to have sold his soul to the Devil at a crossroads in return for his musical skills, before being poisoned by 'person(s) unknown' at the age of 26. Despite his short life, the 41 songs recorded on disc went on to be a huge influence on 1960s and 70s rock stars such as the Rolling Stones and Eric Clapton. Indeed 'Hellhound on my trail' was covered by Fleetwood Mac. Numerous lesser-known (although often more authentically 'blues') musicians have kept Johnson's idiom alive.

But where did Johnson learn of hell hounds? Was this an idea brought to America by European immigrants? Or was it an evolution of African beliefs kept alive within the slave communities? The latter would fit in with the widespread survival of African folklore and beliefs among the black communities in the southern states of America. However, to the best of my knowledge (and this includes two different posts to the FOLKLORE-L email list) there is almost no awareness of phantom black dogs and/or hellhounds among American folklorists (which, I would hasten to add, is not the same as saying there is no such American folklore – clearly the breadth of scope of folklore studies means there are plenty of fruitful areas which simply have not been studied).

So far as I am aware Robert Johnson makes the *only* published reference to hell hounds in the New World. However there are numerous, if decidedly obscure, references to phantom black dogs. The earliest published reference to such entities in America appears to be in Madeleine Vinton Dahlgren's book *South Mountain Magic: A narrative*, published by James B. Osgood in 1882. In 1876 she bought the South Mountain Inn at Turners Gap in Maryland, an area settled mostly by German immigrants. She claims that many witnesses (who she does not name) give a fixed routine and place for the appearance of a dog 'black in colour, of a mystic shining, now waning, now increasing, it crosses the ravine, or disappears like a light suddenly blown out' (page 72). The location of the ravine can be identified and the events take place at the crossroads of what is today known as the National Road and the Zittlestown Road (crossroads are a favourite haunt of British black dogs too; see Bord and Bord 1980, and p53 of this volume). Some of the witnesses said that it had a red mouth, grew larger when attacked, yet was 'airy' when struck at. Interestingly, one person hallucinated '"that *the hill* was coming down on him" which almost paralyzed his faculties so benumbed did he feel' (p80–1). Subsequently a number of other black dog incidents have been reported from Maryland, with repeated sightings near Warfieldsburg between about 1887 and the 1920s. The most recent Maryland sighting known to me happened in 1975 (Chorvinsky 1989).

In their book *Alien Animals* Janet and Colin Bord refer to numerous British black dogs but their New World sightings are restricted to one seen on a farm in the Province of Quebec in 1889 as part of 'poltergeist eruptions' (Bord and Bord 1980: 109) and those reported by Vance Randolph in his 1947 book *Ozark Superstitions.* Randolph's phantom dogs are all from various parts of Missouri. Three are 'ghost dogs' which were shot at (the bullet passed straight through), punched with a fist (the person felt no resistance), had an axe thrown at them (which went through the apparition and hit a tree) or struck with a riding whip (which also passed through). The fourth tale refers to 'a headless phantom dog... thought to live in a hollow elm tree just outside Braggadocio, Missouri, USA.'

The UK magazine *Fortean Times* has an online message board which attracts international contributions, including two separate contributions in October 2001 by the pseudonymous 'blackbelial999':

> I recall an account of a "black dog" appearing in a book about the Bell Witch of Tennessee (U.S. haunting, early 19th century). The book is "Mysterious Spirit: the Bell Witch of Tennessee" by Charles B. Bell & Harriet P. Miller (amazon.com has it). This supposed entity, dubbed the "Bell Witch" could appear in various forms & speak. It terrorized & amazed a 19th cent. community & family (the Bells) in rural U.S. Legend has it that future President Andrew Jackson even witnessed the phenomena. Of course, many skeptics would consider this just folklore. There's a U.S. website you can read this story on, it's bellwitch.org. I think I've seen accounts of mysterious black-dogs also in various occult/strange phenomena encyclopedias & classic ghost stories. Maybe you & your friends just had too much to drink & were easily spooked.
>
> There's a U.S. movie from the 1970s called "Devil Dog." I saw it in the 80s on tv when I was a kid. It has a big, black Chow that's really an ancient demon incarnate. It's a B-grade movie, but you might like it if you're fond of these "mysterious" dog tales.
>
> www.forteantimes.com/forum/showthread.php?s=&threadid=701

The book *Mysterious Spirit: The Bell Witch of Tennessee* by Charles B. Bell and Harriet P. Miller was published in 1985 by Elders Bookstore. A search of Amazon.com reveals that in recent years over ten other books have been published about the Bell Witch; I have no idea if the black dog features in these accounts.

However, with these exceptions, phantom black dogs seem elusive in the annals of New World folklore, and hell hounds are seemingly extinct. I was therefore intrigued when I began receiving a significant number of emails after two preliminary articles about the folklore and mythology of black dogs (Trubshaw 1994a and 1994b) were put online in 1996. Several British-based correspondents added further examples of encounters with phantom black dogs (see www.indigogroup.co.uk/edge/bdemails.htm). More surprising were the emails from people based in America. These emails clearly revealed that the writers' encounters with black dog had been powerful and led to them, many years later, to search the Internet for information. As is often the case with people who have experienced a wide range of 'anomalous phenomena', some were implicitly or explicitly seeking reassurance that they are not suffering from mental instability or delusions.

To allow readers to judge for themselves, here are the most relevant sections of these emails from Americans who have experienced phantom black dogs (see www.indigogroup.co.uk/edge/ bdemails.htm for the full texts). Apart from the descriptions of sightings and lore, these emails also reveal the way books and popular TV programmes have created a limited awareness of American and European phantom black dog lore; in addition there is the somewhat implicit or self-referential way in which the Internet is also increasing such awareness.

While space does not allow a detailed discussion, there is an intriguing aspect to these emails in that they are *exact* records of the witnesses' experiences and feelings (although I have corrected minor errors of spelling and punctuation for this publication; the unedited versions can be found at www.indigogroup.co.uk/edge/bdemails.htm). While technically not orally transmitted, such emails are the next best thing, while also adding a whole new dimension to 'oral' lore in that this is folklore which can be passed on 'in the raw', not mediated through a folklorist's transcriptions and editing, or subjected to the various 'adjustments' inevitably made when such lore is published in more literary formats. This first-hand 'immediacy' gives this chapter a quite different feel to, say, the third-hand accounts of most British sightings.

From Daniel Rolph, December 1999:

> I enjoyed recently reading your article on 'Black Dogs in Folklore,' on the Internet, and thought you may be interested in my own research. Briefly, I finished a Doctorate [in] Folklore years ago, and published a book with the University of Tennessee Press, in 1994, entitled, *To Shoot, Burn, and Hang: Folk History from a Kentucky Mountain Family and Community*. It contains a number of events which transpired in the late 19th and early 20th centuries in the mountain section of Northeastern Kentucky where all my family and I are from, including a 'witch-burning' that transpired there in 1898.
>
> The reason I bring the above to your attention, is in my book, chapter four 'This is the Tree of Justice,' I include the personal experience narrative of my great-grand-father, John E. Rolph, who saw the proverbial, shaggy-haired animal, with

eyes as he said, 'like balls of fire,' about 'the size of a calf,' in 'Rolph Hollow,' (or 'holler' as we say in the Southern Mountain Dialect). He thought he'd seen the Devil, and took it as a token or sign of evil, since that night, a mob broke into the Fleming County, KY jail and took out a man named William Thacker, whom they castrated, tore his tongue out, drove wooden pegs and also pins through his body, drug him behind a horse and finally hung him on a tree near 'Rolph Hollow.' This was in July of 1903.

The 'red-eyed' thing was seen on a number of occasions after this as well in the Hollow. If you can't get the book in England, I'd be more than happy to mail you the chapter, which includes other references (some of which you have in your article) on the 'Black Dog' sightings. My Rolph family and all the families in the area at that time were of English, Scot-Irish ancestry, as are most people in Kentucky. What ever the 'thing' is, it appears to haunt crossroads and appears at the sight or near the place of a murder or where violence has occurred. I tried to place our family's experience in its cultural and ethnic context, but also showed examples outside of that of British lore.

From Donald Panther-Yates [July 2000]:

My wife and I read your article on the web concerning black dogs with great fascination as we had just finished reading *Alien Animals* [(Bord and Bord 1980) – RNT]. We have both seen the phantom black dog, on two different occasions, in Tennessee and Florida. Native American tradition has that it is sent on specific errands from the "master of death." It appeared before a racetrack announcer and a huge crowd in Macon Co., Tenn. about 1920.[...]

You are welcome to pass this information on. It is taken from a book I wrote called *Spirit Giftings*. I am the "first person" in the excerpt, and Chief Paul Russel is "Grandfather." He is 63 years old now and still lives outside Hartsville, Tenn. I have a web address for him if you would like to contact him.

Several years after the Vermont trip I found myself traveling in Tennessee, at the lower end of the Appalachian chain. I was maybe a toddler on the spiritual path by now. It was late in the afternoon on another sunny May day. I had just left the forests of a large state park [Standing Rock, near the border with Kentucky] and was alone in my car. On my left were farmlands and fences with the occasional cabin. On my right was a precipitous hillside with cedars, briars and rock outcroppings. An animal shot across the road in front of me. It appeared to be a large, sleek black dog with long, powerful haunches. But it had a human face with eyes like burning coals. It did not look at me but went straight ahead right up the hillside with a purpose and intensity that chilled me to the bone. It crossed the fence, ditch, road and rocky hillside as though they weren't there.

Shaken, I asked Grandfather about the beast.

'We don't say its name out loud,' he said. 'But it's real. Looking Heart has seen it. So have the children when we lived on the old homestead. It didn't look at you, did it?'

'No.'

'That's good. You'd be dead.'

He told me the story of the Hound of Hell. It was not a true animal. There was only one of its kind. It did not need food to live on. It was not of this earth. It had a master and it would be sent on errands with messages. These were meant for one person, no one else. It could talk.

'It has been seen a lot around Macon County,' he said. 'It appeared at a racetrack around 1920 before several hundred witnesses. That got put in the newspaper [in Red Boiling Springs or Lafayette, Tenn.]. This beast made a beeline and ran directly up to the announcer in his box. It stood up on its hind legs as it approached him, looked him right in the eyes and spoke to him. What it said, no one knows. The man immediately became sick. He went into a coma. He confessed a horrible crime before all those people. He told them he had killed someone many years ago and could not die before confessing it. Then he died. Another case was similar. A man living way back in the woods was visited by this beast. He had secretly murdered his wife and family.'

I never found anyone else who has seen the black dog until I met my wife, Teresa. She will write to you separately of her experience [see below]. We believe the black dog is a

> servant of the 'devil'. Before seeing the black dog I did not believe in this 'devil', being a Native American. The glowing red eyes are its mark and distinguish it from mere 'ghost dogs'.

From Teresa Panther-Yates [July 2000]:

> I believe my husband wrote you separately about the black dog he saw. My daughter Katie and I saw the black dog several years ago before I had met my husband or read about black dogs. This was 1991 or 1992. It was very late at night and we were only yards from my house on a meandering and narrow road. To the right of us was an old fence and bushes and weeds. (There is no water or church nearby that I know of, but that does not mean that there did not used to be.) A huge dog seemed to come from nowhere and jumped in front of the car and lumbered across the fence at an unbelievable speed. At first I thought it a greyhound, but then I realized this was no ordinary dog... it was only the shape of a dog but had no real substance. It was more the shadow of a dog that moved like a dog. The odd thing was how intensely black it truly was – much darker than the dark night outside (for it was truly dark... no street lights).
>
> It sent a chill up my spine and I froze in fear. I asked my daughter if she saw it (she has also been able to see what you can call spirits or ghosts before as I have, but nothing like this). She said in a very quiet frozen voice, 'Yes, and I never want to speak of it again... '
>
> I did not see its eyes and I am glad from what I have read of it, and I pray I never see it again. It seemed to have some demonic and sure purpose in its intense speed and straight direction and the feeling that we both had about it. I have determined it is the messenger of the devil from all of this.

From Michael Perry [September 2000]:

> My name is Michael Perry and I live in Atlanta, Georgia. I was watching the Discovery channel and they had a show on about 'haunted animals'. One of the animals was the Black Dog. I was so drawn to the show and the people they interviewed that had encountered these dogs were definitely not actors. They did the story of the church on that stormy

night when the dog had came in and killed some people. On the door where the dog had came in, there were burn marks on it [Bungay? – RNT]. It also said that the bells at the top of the chapel would get rid of any 'satanic' creatures. Three people ran up the tower to ring the bells but lightning on that stormy night killed all three of them. It also said if you saw one of these dogs you could not tell anyone for one year and one day, or someone in your family will die.

Between the show and your report, I am convinced that these dogs are for real. [Whether] they are all coincidence that members of their family die shortly after seeing these dogs, or these dogs are truly haunted, I don't know.

From Cindy Fallon [February 2002]:

I was listening to Art Bell's 'Coast to Coast' on the radio the other night. A police officer in South Carolina called in to share his account from years ago of his encounter with what he called a 'demonic dog'. He said it just appeared in his bedroom and he was sure he would die as it walked towards him and looked right at him. All he could do was close his eyes and pray. Described as 'big' with a 'matted coat', he likened it to the rabid St Bernard in Stephen King's *Cujo*. He kept saying 'it smelt like death'. Being a police officer, he insisted he knew what death smells like. He insisted the dog was REAL. Chills ran up my neck as I listened to his account. Although he did not specify color, I immediately envisioned the Black Dog known as 'Shuck' from his description. He asked the host if anyone has ever heard of such a thing. Moments later, another listener told Art Bell about 'Black Shuck'. The officer said he's never heard of such stories before, and neither had Art Bell. Now that someone came forward on this show, I wouldn't be surprised to hear others call in. I was so excited to continue to find other modern witnesses, I couldn't sleep!

From Cindy Fallon [April 2002]:

I always loved visiting my father as a preteen in the late 1980s. Dad rented a room in a house set back in the woods of Suffolk County, Long Island, in New York. A long hidden dirt road driveway took us past another house before reaching the dirt cul-de-sac in front of the house where my father lived. I loved that house, the woods, and all of the animals to watch there – wild and domestic. I love animals and Nature places, and such things never evoked any kind of fear in me. I loved playing with the guard Rottweiler, Ben, every visit.

One late Summer afternoon, Dad sent me out to retrieve something for him that was in his car. I innocently walked onto the dirt cul-de-sac. The Rottweiler, "Ben," remained on the porch behind me. All of a sudden, in the clearness of the afternoon sun, I saw this *enormous black dog-like* creature come charging out of the woods to my right a few yards in front of me. I can't honestly say if it truly came from the woods or merely 'manifested' at that point because I was not looking at that exact spot until the creature caught my attention by coming into my view. I can't overemphasize the word 'dog-like' enough because it was obviously not a true dog like the Rott behind me, nor was it like anything I had ever seen or imagined in my lifetime before or since. It was grossly larger than a real dog (300–400+ lbs?), more massive than a Mastiff, and 'ran' with a most unusual, exaggerated gait – not like a dog at all – or any other animal for that matter. There was something undog-like about its haunches or hind legs and the way they moved as it 'ran' across the dirt driveway and cul-de-sac. I can't pinpoint what about its hind legs was so unsettling to me, other than to say the beast's gait was out of the ordinary of any animal, lame or healthy. I'm not even sure if its feet ever truly touched the ground because it made no sound – not of feet, of breath, or of any other animal sounds. In unnatural silence, it 'ran' across the dirt driveway and behind the circle of scant trees and shrubs of the cul-de-sac. I could still see the black dog-like beast behind the thin foliage as it was now on the other side of the dirt cul-de-sac.

As my eyes continued to follow it, the rest of my body remained frozen in absolute fear. I was totally captivated in horror and disbelief of this creature that I tuned out the rest of the world for these brief moments as this terror demanded my total attention. I could see it continue onto the other side of the driveway cul-de-sac in a straight line perpendicular to me. The creature never once looked in my direction or even seemed to notice that I even existed in the same world as it.

(For that, I am thankful for I'm afraid I would have died of fright if it had looked at me!) It never changed its direction – as if it knew where it was going or needed to be – hell-bent on its course. It just continued in the straight line it was running on until it disappeared – and I don't mean it retreated into the woods – I mean it *vanished* into air before leaving the driveway for the other side of the woods! Throughout the entire event, I stood petrified in absolute terror, innately knowing what I had just witnessed was no animal of *this* world. Once it disappeared into nothingness, I came out of my spellbound horror and immediately turned to retreat back into the house, never making it to the car where I was at first headed when I first caught sight of the black dog-like beast.

When I turned to go back into the house after the creature disappeared, the Rottweiler who had always been so friendly with me now stood on the porch snarling, growling, and backing up as if he was about to attack. My back was now towards the area where I had just seen the creature running. Was beloved Ben truly growling at *me* or was he also seeing the creature that had by now disappeared from my sight? I will never know. Ben would not let me pass and enter the house. I called out to my dad that Ben wouldn't let me in, but he didn't realize how threatening the Rott was acting and called out from inside the house that I should, 'Just walk around him.' I assured my dad that was not possible, so he walked out onto the porch and 'Ben' immediately calmed down and I was allowed to pass and re-enter the house.

As soon as I was inside, I told my father what I had just witnessed that left me so horrified. I called it a 'Black Dog' for lack of a better description but was very clear about the fact it was not a true dog at all. I assure you I had never heard of a 'Black Dog' before I named the creature I witnessed that, myself. I have never been back to that house since that last visit when I was a preteen. Dad comes to visit me, now, and he himself had to move after a terrible accident 6 months later at that house (in the cul-de-sac driveway no less!) where he had to be brought back to life by paramedics. (I never believed my sighting and his accident were related in any way because I did not perceive the Black Dog as an omen so much as a thing of horror.) After the accident, Dad had to move away from that area of Suffolk County, New York.

Now in my mid-20s, I've been looking more into Black Dog phenomenon for a better understanding of the beast that ran into my life bringing terror years earlier. I'm astonished how widespread and *old* the phenomenon is and am stunned that modern sightings, like my own, still continue to come in. Some researchers theorize that Black Dog activity is often tied to specific land features. This revelation led me to ask my father a series of questions about the land his old house was on and any 'untimely deaths' on the land. I hadn't mentioned at first my questions were tied to my Black Dog sighting for fear he might not take my inquisition seriously. He was curious about my line of questions, so I at last refreshed his memory about my Black Dog experience during my last visit. We hadn't spoken of it since it occurred years earlier. I recapped what I had witnessed that day for him, still breathless as I recalled the event from so long ago. He said he distinctly remembers my fear from that very day. I told him that I have been reading lately that Black Dogs, like the one I encountered, as most often associated with dirt roads, wells, or ley lines. His interest peaked when he told me we had *all* of those land features there. My encounter was on the dirt road driveway and dirt cul-de-sac. He confirmed a well on the grounds, just yards from my encounter. He then went further to say that there were cemeteries on either side of the property, out of view, but close in the vicinity, no less. After our phone conversation, he e-mailed me some maps of the area of the house where I saw the Black Dog. The house was in a *direct line* between an ancient Native American burial ground and a 19th century church and cemetery. He sent another map that showed the house was aligned *exactly* 1.41 miles from the Native American burial ground to the Northeast and *exactly* 1.41 miles from the old cemetery to the Southwest. The property was in the *exact middle* of the aligned burial grounds. All of these things were news to me, but fit right in with the theory that most Black Dogs occur in such areas.

Also interesting to note, there was a murder on the property. This, too, was shocking news to me! I don't blame my father for never wanting to tell me this when I was a child, but as an adult, he knows that I did encounter something on the property he can't deny. My father did not live on the property at the time of the murder, so he only remembers it from the landlord's accounts, but there is no doubt a murder was committed on the property. Dad and I don't know where the body was buried.

From Joseph Pyne [June 2002]:

> I am a resident of Hagerstown, Maryland in the United States. Legends of spectral black dogs still exist here even to this day. It was often a favorite 'ghost story' told by my grandparents when they were still alive. My mother still speaks of stories on occasion. Local folklore of this area, and surrounding areas such as Boonsboro and South Mountain, claims that seeing the black dog can be a harbinger of death. My grandfather claimed to have seen it several times, but did not reach his end until years later. The most vivid story I can recall is when he said he was coming home off the mountain and saw a large black dog standing in the middle of the road. He was driving his pick-up truck home in the evening. With no time to stop, he said he ran over it, feeling and hearing a 'thump' as he rolled over the dog's body. He stopped and looked back, only to see the dog still standing there. It was staring at him, then growled and vanished into the evening air. My grandmother, a few weeks before she died in her bed, even claimed that a black dog came into to her room at night and crawled beneath her bed. The folklore in this area is quite strong among the older generation, and still important to those of us who may be young but still remember.
>
> P.S. The black dog is often called the 'Snarly Yow' around these parts.

This reference to Snarly Yow indicates that American lore has been influenced by Frederick Marryat's book *Snarley-Yow or the Dog-fiend*, published in 1837 or books which cite this work, such as William Dutt's, *Highways and Byways of East Anglia* (1901) or James Wentworth Day's *In Search of Ghosts* (1969). The name Snarleyow seems to have been quite common in nineteenth century Britain for dogs and, less commonly, horses and ships(!).

From C. E. De Rosett [September 2002]:

> I have had some experiences with the Black Dog. My experiences began about forty-three years ago.
>
> I dreamed one night of a white horse who was very large and frightening. I told my mother of the dream and she told me it meant that there would soon be a death. She seemed terribly shaken. Within two weeks of the dream a close friend died. I don't remember ever dreaming of the white horse again.
>
> I then began to have dreams of a 'demon dog', medium size, black, with glowing red eyes. These dreams were terrifying. I truly thought I had been face to face with a demon. Through out the years the pattern has been that within two weeks of the dreams someone I felt closely bonded with would die, an infant sister-in-law, uncles and aunts as well as some close friends.
>
> A day or two before the birth of my son I dreamed of the dog again. In this dream the dog was a small pup who lay outside my bedroom window and was ill. In this dream I realized that without care the dog would die. Knowing just what dog this was I was tempted to let it die. I was unable to do that though and decided I must go outside, get the dog and nurse it back to health. This dream was not at all pleasant. I had much fear yet managed to care for the dog in spite of the overwhelming fear. I awakened knowing the dog would survive. I believe I came to understand the purpose of the dream about a week later, June 1, 1962, the day of my son's birth. My son was ill at birth, internal haemorrhaging, and not expected to survive. He did survive and is now forty years of age.
>
> Then one evening, one month and four days after the birth of my son, I saw the dog with my physical eyes. My husband and had been watching television. I headed to the bathroom. I'm wide awake and on my feet when I saw the dog seated on the bedroom floor at the foot of my bed. He was as real, as solid, as any thing physical. I could not see through him as one might see through a 'ghost'. I stopped, shocked to see a dog in the house. I looked at him and became terrified. I recognized who he was. His red glowing eyes somehow captured my attention. I could not move nor make a sound. It

was as though I was stuck in that spot. He looked at me intensely, eye to eye. Once I acknowledged who he was and that he was there to forewarn of death, he turned his head slightly. He was no longer looking at me. He looked like a dog who is saddened, head turned slightly away and down. In that instant he faded away. I thought I would not tell my husband and took my time returning to the living room believing I had regained my composure. He looked at me and said, "You look like you've just seen a ghost!" I then told him what had happened. I also explained that I felt as though I had come face to face with the devil himself. Neither of us understood why he appeared in physical form until the following day when my four-year old daughter died.

I continue to dream of the dog on occasion and always with the expected results. I prayed to have this 'curse' removed. It was such a terrifying experience I did not want any part of it. I wanted never again to have this experience, even to forget it had ever happened. I really thought the whole thing was evil. I thought that I had been evil because I had dabbled in the occult, Ouija Board and Scrying out of curiosity, and this was my punishment. In time I thought my mind had created this dog and therefore could get rid of it.

About eight years ago I saw him again with my physical eyes. On this particular morning I awakened feeling as thought I hadn't slept enough. I lay in bed for a moment before feeling ready to get up and prepare to go to work. As I turned to get out of bed I saw the dog sitting there. He was like any dog sitting on the floor at the side of the bed. We were nose to nose! Again there was this intense eye contact, recognition of who he is, and what he had come to inform me about. I felt the usual terror. I noticed his eyes were glowing as usual but this time yellow and not red. He faded away. I also thought there was something else different about him this time. I just could not identify what that something was. I though he had come for me this time, that I would be the person to die. I decided this time I'd say nothing to my children. I did share this with two friends.

My youngest daughter was planning to move back to Arizona from California and would be renting a U-Haul truck for the move. I hoped I would not die before seeing her again. One night about midnight she telephoned from her sister's home in Prescott, about forty-five miles from my home. She said she and her fiancé were leaving there within a short time to come to my home. I feared for their safety so suggested they not come until morning after they'd had a night's rest. They had been driving for about eight hours and which ever of the two possible routes they would take they would have to come down some steep and winding mountain roads. I was very much afraid for them. I just didn't want to alarm them by saying anything about having seen 'the dog'. She insisted they would arrive at my home in less than an hour. I could not talk her out of this until I said to her that I had seen 'the dog'. Immediately she said "Oh, OK Mom. We'll stay here tonight. We'll see you tomorrow." As she and her fiancé had planned to shop around for a used auto while in Arizona they went to a car lot, in Prescott, the following day after unloading the truck. As they pulled into the car lot something fell out of the U Haul truck, the axle! I believe the dog came with a warning and that warning saved lives this time.

In the meantime my oldest daughter began seeing the dog. Just before the death of her grandmother and just before the death of her father. She shared that when she first encountered him she thought – "No, he can't be here. That's Mom's dog." She also reports there is much terror associated with his appearance.

My granddaughter is also having these experiences. She reports she has seen him yet usually simply senses his presence. She has reported this to her mother every time it has happened and each time there has been a death.

Thinking I should never have told my children about the black dog, I blamed myself for this. For many years I referred to him as "the black dog", "the demon dog", or "*the* dog".

Until August 26, 1992, I had never known others have experienced the Black Dog. I know the date because I had made a note of this and today (Sept. 17, 2002) I found the note. I then began to realize this dog is not a creation of my mind. He is an entity with a mind and a will of his own. That made him even more frightening to me.

> I have often wondered what is the point of him showing himself to me? I don't know who will die, I can't do anything to prevent the death. I do now, however, pray that the person whose death he has predicted will pass peacefully without pain and fear.
>
> I must add that without his appearance at the time of my daughter's move from California though, I might have lost another loved one, my youngest child.

From Liz Willow [October 2002]:

> I've been researching the "black dog" phenomena for a while. I've also heard that they can also be a psychopomp (a messenger or something that takes the soul to its afterlife) as well as an omen for death. The reason it is so interesting is that while I knew a bit about it my mother did not. Shortly before and after my father died she has seen a black dog wandering around the neighbor's yard and she says "staring over the fence at her." She saw it again the other day and we received news last evening that my Uncle had died that day. I've been able to somewhat explain the myth to her but obviously... it's not a myth for her now. I don't have an explanation as to why we would be seeing it *now* within the last couple of years as opposed to any other times of death in the family.
>
> We live in Glen Carbon, Illinois, USA and as far as I know have no ties to England where the dog seems to be seen the most often.

From Melie [January 2003] :

> This is the first time I have heard anything on black dogs. But I have seen one. I am 50 years old now but when I was 6 or 7 I was helping my grandma in her little store. She used to make and sell corn tortialas and tamales. Well anyway it was getting dark and I was getting scared cause I had to go thru a cemetary to get to my house. So I was upset with grandma for keeping me so long. I started to go out the door, I opened the door and there it was a big black dog with red eyes. We stared at each other. I was so scared I couldn't move. I yell, went back inside and told my grandma. She went to the door, open it and call out to the dog, but the dog never

> showed up again. All this time I have been thinking I must have dreamed it. But I know I was awake.
>
> P.S. My grandma lived in Pharr. That's in the Rio Grande Valley, south Texas. The cemetary was one block away.

And, to add a Caribbean example of black dog lore, this email from Kenneth Lowe [October 2002]:

> I am a student of Afro-Caribbean background (Trinidad) now studying in the UK. [...] This is a synopsis of a story related to me by my mother who was born and raised on the island of Grenada, 100 miles north of Trinidad.
>
> When she was a child she often spent weekends at her grandmother's house (this was just after World War II). Early one morning she set out to walk back home to her mother's house with her grandmother, this route took them through unlit cocoa plantations and rural roads with only starlight to guide them. My mother tells me that on passing a local shop that she knew well she saw a huge white dog sleeping in front of its locked front door. Interestingly enough, the dog did not give any indication that it was aware of their presence and her grandmother did not seem to pay much attention to it.
>
> The incident that remains embedded in her memory occurred just as her mother's house came into view. Her grandmother always wore a wide brimmed straw hat and my mother said that she distinctly remembers a "sound like that of gravel falling on the brim of mama's hat" after which she was heard to say to someone (or something) "Yuh goin? Byebye" (Translation: "You're off? OK fine, goodbye"), as if she was talking to an old friend. She says that she later heard her grandmother say to her mother that the dog was a guardian that protected her whenever she walked alone at night. I have heard of other similar stories involving canine apparitions in the Caribbean; they may be worth investigating.

From Scott Vancouver (December 2003)

> I have been interested in 'The Black Dog' sightings since hearing of my uncle's 'imaginary friend'. He describes the creature from his youth with great detail, even today.

Initially he was very frightened of the beast (due to it's appearance) but as his 'visits' became more frequent he learned to think of it as a friend and a protector (I don't know if the creature spoke to him but he speaks of receiving reassurance from his friend that he would not harm him). His friend also had a name: Docky-Doo and is described as being a large black dog (blacker than night that forms from the shadows of the periphery) about the size of a calf (my family is rural). The dog had great paws and fiery, glowing red eyes (This is of course is the dominant feature described by my uncle).

My uncle's Docky-Doo had one feature that differs from other sightings I have read about in that it's mouth opened sideways. No one else in the large family saw the Docky-Doo at that time (or admits to it) and I have no knowledge of any family tragedy at that time (which isn't to say that there wasn't any as this happened long before I was even thought of).

The only other person to have witnessed a similar creature is my cousin some 30 odd years our uncle's junior. This would have been sometime in the seventies or eighties. My cousin's description as a child is exactly like my uncle's (right down to the sideways mouth and it being scary looking but still a friend), everything is the same except the name: Eeo (E-oh).

Just thought you might like to know that there has been sightings in my home region (Rural Central Alberta, Canada).

From Lise (December 2004)

Hello

I finally can rest assured that I was not hallucinating one very windy summer night twenty years ago when living at my parents house in Bouctouche, New-Brunswick, Canada.

I always told people my story about the Black Dog apparition I experienced, yet I never had any explanation for what happened until now, nor did I realize this was an actual phenomenon that happened to individuals other than myself.

Here's my account of the events:

I was a very hot summer night, I couldn't sleep, and it was just too uncomfortable upstairs where my bedroom was in my parents 100-year-old house. My mother, being the night owl that she is was still awake and I knew she would be downstairs so I got up. It was around midnight when I got up, went downstairs and told my mother I was going outside to sit on the front step for a breath of fresh air.

I went outside and was sitting on the steps, the wind was blowing the trees all over the place and it was a little spooky, but I needed to cool off. I looked down for a few seconds when a chill went down my spine and I had this horrible feeling someone or something was watching me. Slowly I raised my head and there It was, staring at me, not moving, just sitting a few feet away from me. Just writing this I can picture him, the unblinking eyes, the big black body.... Anyways, needless to say, I was scared out of my tree, I was just too scared to move! What do I do? I start saying the Our Father, thinking if the Dog was something evil, the prayer will make him go away... Again, looking down for not even a second, he just vanished out of thin air the same way he came!!!! I was frozen from fear, with this feeling of... I can't even explain it.

I ran inside the house and when my mother saw my face, she asked me what happened because she said I was as white as a sheet when she looked at me! I then proceeded to explain to her the encounter.

To this day when I come home at night I still cannot look directly in front of me when I come up the drive way and park. I just look sideways towards the door for fear of seeing the Black Dog again. I have chills every time I tell someone about what happened to me that night.

PS: As far as the Black Dog itself, from what I read on your site it appears to different people in various shapes and sizes. Mine reminded me more of a Black Lab[rador], but it was surely not the friendly type. It was big, menacing, sitting there staring at me in silence. I really didn't get a good look at his eyes thinking in my head that if you stare down a dog it will surely attack because it feels provoked, so I can't say they were red. If I had to say anything about them they did shine,

> but that could have been like any other animal's eyes at night....

What do all these emails tell us about phantom black dogs in America? Well, they strongly suggest such entities are thriving! There are parallels with British black dog lore, for example the tendency to regard sightings as portents of death. Unsurprisingly, some witnesses frame their outlook of the experience according to Christian concepts of good, evil, the Devil, etc..

Joseph Pyne confirms that black dog lore is widely-known in Maryland and adds that such creatures have their own name, the Snarly Yow. Donald Panther-Yates refers to native American lore about black dogs (although the parallels to Daniel Rolph's published account are surprisingly close) and Kenneth Lowe provides clear evidence for such lore being well-established in Trinidad. However this is the only evidence these emails offer for an oral tradition. Literary versions of the lore (excluding the Internet) are seemingly restricted to three specialist books (Daniel Rolph's *To Shoot, Burn, and Hang*; Donald Panther-Yates' *Spirit Giftings*; and Janet and Colin Bord's *Alien Animals*). Unsurprisingly, none of these witnesses recall reading the two earlier books (Madeleine Vinton Dahlgren's *South Mountain Magic;* Vance Randolph's *Ozark Superstitions)* or Mark Chorvinsky's brief account of Maryland black dogs in the September 1989 issue of *Fate*.

However, although written references to phantom black dogs in the New World are sparse, these emails reveal that black dog lore has been disseminated in the popular media – Art Bell's 'Coast to Coast' radio show and the Discovery channel are specifically mentioned in the emails, but are unlikely to be the only instances.

In December 2004 I Googled for various permutations of 'black dog' and American magazines such as *Strange* and *Fate*. Also fairly well-known in America was a book-format reprint of the UK part-work magazine *The Unexplained*; this brought to light one another example of a phantom black dog tale, this time from Texas:

> 'Ed Koehler, a reader of *The Unexplained* Site, tells of a very strange encounter with a black dog while working as a security guard in Dallas, Texas in 1983. Late at night, Ed began to see a very tall man out of the corner of his eye as his partner saw a black hound. Later, Koehler learned the building was built a top [i.e. on top of] a farm in which a man, his wife and dog had been killed.'

('Cassiel Sophia' c.2002–3; www.meta-religion.com/Paranormale/Cryptozoology/Canine/black_dogs.htm)

I have been unable to locate the part of *The Unexplained* site where Ed Koehler posted his message and suspect that this is no longer online.

Despite Googling with various permutations of 'black dog', 'the unexplained', 'fate' and 'strange' I was unable to come up with any further online references to phantom black dogs being discussed in *The Unexplained, Fate* or *Strange* magazines. This suggests there is limited awareness of black dog folklore in America, making Art Bell's 'Coast to Coast' programme in February 2002 referred to by Cindy Fallon one of the few exceptions.

As Jeremy Harte has argued in the opening chapter of the present volume, the concept of black dog folklore seems to have evolved in Britain during the last two hundred years, so perhaps the limited awareness of this lore in the New World should not be surprising. Nevertheless the hell hound of Robert Johnston's 1930s blues and the Snarly Yow of Maryland reported by Joseph Pyne suggest that black dog lore is – or was – a little-known aspect of New World lore, albeit not referred to by the term 'phantom black dog'.

Nevertheless, if even if there is a reasonably widespread (although low level) awareness of phantom black dogs in America, apparently spontaneous sightings such as that reported by Cindy Fallon are difficult to consider 'merely' as folklore. As Simon Sherwood's chapter in the present volume has indicated, we should be looking at the interaction between relevant psychological, physiological and environmental aspects. Given the limited awareness of black dog folklore in the New World then it could be easier to separate the psychological, physiological and environmental aspects than in Britain.

Acknowledgements

My grateful thanks to all the email correspondents for giving permission to publish their accounts. I am especially grateful to Janet Bord for sharing her information about Maryland examples. Thanks also to Mike Shoemaker who brought Madeleine Dahlgren's *South Mountain Magic* to the attention of Janet Bord, and Jeremy Harte for the Snarleyow details.

The Black Dog in England: A bibliography

Jeremy Harte

There is an extensive literature on the Black Dog and allied topics – the earliest accounts date from classical antiquity, while modern ones can be found across the world. This survey is restricted to modern England only, beginning with the early folklorists in 1800. It has been organised in two sections. The first is set out by county, and lists all known references to Black Dogs, whether as unattributed traditions or personal experiences, followed by a motif index. The second section, in date order, lists all individual encounters with Black Dogs recorded from this period.

Conventional county boundaries have been used, rather than the administrative ones created in 1974 or 1992. Accounts from Uplyme and Lyme Regis, which lie on the Devon/Dorset border, have been reckoned with Dorset. Many accounts of Black Dogs contain material repeated from earlier sources, but for this survey, traditions and experiences are indexed only under their first appearance in print.

Following each geographical reference, there is a note on the typical imagery that it uses to describe the Black Dog. This follows the order in the motif index, as given at the end of this section, although the motifs may appear in a different order in the initial source. The original references are, of course, much richer than this bald summary can suggest. One source may refer to a single tradition, another may cover dozens, from many different places. Some authors offer a bald summary, while others are master storytellers. A survey like this can only offer an introduction.

Local Traditions

Bedfordshire: Smith 1904: 163–4 (at gates, headless, dangerous to touch); Rickard 1981: 45 (accompanies traveller).

Berkshire: Miles 1907–8: 259 (glowing eyes, big as a calf, walks on hindlegs); Barham 1973: 16 (howling).

Buckinghamshire: Chambers 1864: 2.433 (at gate, glowing eyes, blow goes through, dangerous to touch); Tebbult 1945 (accompanies vehicle, vanishes).

Cambridgeshire: Taylor 1850 (at churchyard, appears at midnight, glowing eyes, big as a calf, shaggy, explodes); Miss Baker c1950 in Oates and Wood 1998: 59 (glowing eyes, shaggy, walks on hindlegs); Day 1954: 21–5 and 1958: 200 (glowing eyes, big as a calf, attacks people, portends death); Porter 1969: 53 (with chain, portends death); Bunn 1977a (at water, vanishes); Brooks 1994: 105; 'Wiccawillow' 2004 (portends death).

Cheshire: Hole 1937: 163 (at water, runs a route, accompanies traveller, glowing eyes, sound of footsteps, blow goes through, vanishes, attacks people).

Cornwall: Crowe 1848: 341 (in house, portends death); Spooner 1925–30a (at bridge, at water, runs a route, big as a calf, explodes, vanishes); Spooner 1925–30b (at bridge, runs a route, glowing eyes, big as a calf, headless, vanishes, throws people down, ghost of accident victim); Brown 1962: 27–8 (in house, vanishes); Deane and Shaw 1975: 73 (glowing eyes, big as a calf, ghost of accident victim).

Cumberland: Sullivan 1857: 156 (vanishes, ghost of suicide); Findler 1979: 61–2 (portends death).

Derbyshire: Addy 1895: 137 (at crossroads, glowing eyes, visible to one only, headless, portends death); Pegge 1896: 4 (glowing eyes, big as a calf, dangerous to touch); MacGregor 1955: 162–4 (walks through walls); Daniel 1973: 44–6 (at crossroads, accompanies travellers, glowing eyes, visible to one only, soundless tread, blow goes through, walks through walls, vanishes, portends misfortune, portends death, 'guardian dog' tale type); Clarke 1991: 75–6 (at water, runs a route, headless, portends death); Clarke 2000: 59–62, 91 (howling, invisible, vanishes).

Devon: Bray 1838: 2.299–300 (in house, glowing eyes, vanishes); 'R.J.K.' 1850: 512 (headless); 'M' 1870 (at bridge, runs a route, appears at midnight); Doe 1880: 100 (accompanies vehicle, vanishes); Baring-Gould 1892: 5 (at churchyard); Hewett 1900: 39–41 (at crossroads, runs a route, accompanies traveller, big as a calf, sound of footsteps, blow goes through, explodes, throws people down, ghost of murder victim); Chope 1927: 161, Day 1958: 204–17 and Harte 1995 (runs a route, accompanies traveller, accompanies vehicle, glowing eyes, big as a calf, howling, vanishes, vanishes when run over); Chope 1928: 117–9 (accompanies traveller, blow goes through, vanishes); Chope 1936: 87–8 (in house, walks on hindlegs, vanishes, ghost of murder victim); Brown 1955: 358 (big as a calf, headless, portends misfortune); Brown 1959 (in house, appears at midnight, big as a calf, howling); Brown 1964: 96; St.Leger-Gordon 1965: 36–40 (vanishes); Brown 1978a: 217 (at gate, accompanies vehicle, big as a calf, walks on hindlegs); Farson 1978: 30 and Brown 1985: 241–2 (vanishes when run over); Brown 1982: 113–9 (accompanies traveller, big as a calf, shaggy, vanishes, 'guardian dog' tale type); Innes 1983a, 1983b (in house, glowing eyes, dangerous to touch, explodes); Rickard 1983: 53–5 (big as a calf); Beer 1984: 30–3 (big as a calf, vanishes, vanishes when run over); Brown 1988: 229; Clark 1993: 400 (vanishes when run over); Williamson 1995 (at churchyard, blow goes through).

Dorset: William Barnes 1844 in Barnes 1962: 1.186 (dangerous to touch); Chambers 1864: 2.434 and Larwood and Hotten 1866: 193 (appears at midnight, big as a calf, visible to one only); Rogers 1926: 135 (accompanies travellers); Dacombe 1935: 115–6 (runs a route, with chain, invisible, blow goes through, vanishes); 'M.E.R.' 1955–6: 120 (runs a route, with chain); Bond 1956: 112; Brown 1959: 42 (appears at midnight, with chain); Parke 1963: 486 (in house, glowing eyes, blow goes through, vanishes); Waring 1966 (at gate, in house, runs a route, glowing eyes, big as a calf, with chain, walks on hindlegs, portends death); Aylott 1969 (howling, headless); Palmer 1973: 126–7 (at bridge, runs a route, with chain, invisible); Waring 1973: 1–11 (at churchyard, runs a route, accompanies traveller, accompanies vehicle, headless); Gant 1980: 65 (runs a route); Brown 1982: 119; Barrett 1985: 102 (with chain); Harte 1986: 41 (portends death); Durston 1987: 1–5 (glowing eyes, big as a calf, attacks people); see also North 2003.

Durham: Joseph Ritson 1803 in Ritson 1831: 58 (howling); Longstaffe 1854: 13–14 (big as a calf); Brockie 1886: 47–51, 52–5, 59–60 (accompanies travellers, howling, portends misfortune, ghost of accident victim); Hare 1896–1900: 5.425 ('guardian dog' tale type); Brown 1970: 7 ('guardian dog' tale type)

Essex: Newman and Wilson 1952: 100 (portends death); Day 1954: 30, 1958: 201 and 1973: 11–12 (accompanies vehicle, glowing eyes, big as a calf); Brown 1958: 187 (explodes, dangerous to touch); Maple 1964: 186 (accompanies traveller, vanishes); Day 1969: 151–3 (accompanies cyclist, big as a calf, shaggy); Bunn 1977a (vanishes, portends death); Bunn 1981 (glowing eyes, portends death); Goss 1992a: 201; Goss 1992b (at churchyard, vanishes when run over); Jennings 1994 (vanishes when run over).

Gloucestershire: Partridge 1912: 340 (accompanies traveller, invisible); Green 1973: 122 (at water, headless); Briggs 1974: 75; Farson 1978: 31 (headless, vanishes); Turner 1993: 175 (at gate, walks through walls); Palmer 1994: 155 (at water, accompanies traveller, vanishes).

Hampshire: Beddington and Christy 1937: 121–2 (invisible, sound of footsteps); Smith 1938 (in house, vanishes); Sanders 1984: 4 (at water, big as a calf).

Herefordshire: Leather 1912: 38–9 (at water, accompanies vehicle, with chain, vanishes); Woodley 1994 (at churchyard, vanishes).

Hertfordshire: Chambers 1864: 2.434 (glowing eyes, big as a calf, vanishes); Oates and Wood 1998: 39 (big as a calf, shaggy).

Isle of Wight: Rae-Ellis 1990: 91–3 (leaves no footprints, saves from danger); Baldwin 1992: 17–18 (vanishes when run over).

Kent: Dickens 1861: 234 (walks on hindlegs, portends death); Day 1954: 31–3 (in house, walks through walls, vanishes, portends death); Bord and Bord 1987: 49 and Parish 1998: 81 (vanishes); Tudor 2004 (big as a calf); see also Arnold 2003.

Lancashire: Wilkinson 1850 (at churchyard, at water, glowing eyes, shaggy, invisible, sound of footsteps, blow goes through, vanishes, portends death); Jackson 1855: 98 ('guardian dog' tale type); Harland and Wilkinson 1867: 51–6 (at water, in house, glowing eyes); Hardwick 1872: 172 (at bridge, howling, headless, portends misfortune); Bowker 1883: 27–36 (at bridge, appears at midnight, accompanies traveller, glowing eyes, shaggy, howling, sound of footsteps, blow goes through, portends death; may derive from Wilkinson 1850); Wilkinson and Tattersall 1889: 60–1, Wilkinson

1904–5: 4–5 (vanishes); Taylor 1901 s.v. Bargaist; Newman and Wilson 1952: 98–9 (appears at midnight, headless, portends death); Brown 1962: 28 (portends death); Brown 1970: 8 (in house, vanishes, portends death); Brooks 1994: 183 (leaves no footprints); Billingsley 1997 (vanishes when run over); Fields 1998: 6, 38 (glowing eyes, headless, vanishes, portends death); Jeffrey 2004 (at water, headless, walks through walls).

Leicestershire: Nichols 1795–1815: 4ii.970 (at bridge, at gate, shaggy, vanishes); Swift 1954: 60–5 (at water, accompanies travellers, glowing eyes, with chain, 'guardian dog' tale type); Palmer 1985: 197 (glowing eyes, portends misfortune); Bell 1992 (big as a calf, portends death).

Lincolnshire: Peacock 1877: 31, Peacock 1894–5: 146–7 and Peacock 1898 (at churchyard, attacks people); Gutch and Peacock 1908: 53–6 (glowing eyes, attacks people); Welby 1934–5: 132–3; Johnson 1936–7: 83 (glowing eyes); Rudkin 1938 (at churchyard, at water, in house, accompanies traveller, accompanies cyclist, glowing eyes, big as a calf, shaggy, invisible, soundless tread, walks on hindlegs, blow goes through, vanishes, ghost of murder victim, ghost of suicide); Rudkin 1955: 390–1 (accompanies cyclist, vanishes, 'guardian dog' tale type); Wiltshire 1984: 18 (accompanies traveller, vanishes); Miller 1984 (at bridge, at gate, at water, in house, appears at midnight, accompanies cyclist, glowing eyes, big as a calf, with chain, invisible, sound of footsteps, walks through walls, vanishes, vanishes when run over, portends death, ghost of murder victim); Baldwin-Ives 1991; Needle 2001 (accompanies traveller, vanishes); Sherwood 2002 (in house, glowing eyes, vanishes).

Norfolk: Forby 1830: 2.238 (big as a calf, throws people down); Gunn 1849: 300, 307 (runs a route, glowing eyes, headless, blow goes through); Taylor 1850 (at churchyard, appears at midnight, glowing eyes, big as a calf, shaggy, explodes); 'T.D.P.' 1864 (runs a route, glowing eyes, headless, portends misfortune); Barkley 1872 (glowing eyes, portends misfortune, portends death); Rye 1872–3: 2 (at bridge, glowing eyes, big as a calf, shaggy, headless); Rye 1877: 293 (glowing eyes, portends death); Suffling 1891: 106–7 (glowing eyes, with chain, portends death); James 1891: 9–11 (at churchyard, big as a calf, visible to one only, sound of footsteps); Hare 1896–1900: 6.303–4 (at water, in house); Haggard 1899: 26; Cranworth 1900–1: 170–1 (runs a route, glowing eyes, big as a calf, shaggy, vanishes); Thelwall 1900–1: 297 (big as a calf); Mackie 1904–5: 105 (glowing eyes, shaggy, howling, headless); Kent 1910: 111 (glowing eyes, shaggy, sound of footsteps, attacks people); Adams 1914: 126–8, 187–92 (at churchyard, accompanies travellers, glowing eyes, sound of footsteps, soundless tread, walks through walls, vanishes, attacks people, portends misfortune; may derive from James 1891: 9–11); Rye 1920: 28 (glowing eyes, big as a calf, throws people down); Marlowe 1927: 190, 198–204 (howling, attacks people); Hole 1940a: 150 (walks on hindlegs, portends death); Day 1954: 26–30 (vanishes when run over); MacGregor 1955: 64–7 (vanishes, vanishes when run over); Day 1958: 201, 203–4 (runs a route, vanishes when run over); Day 1962: 640 (at bridge, sound of footsteps, walks through walls); Randell 1966: 99–100 (with chain, leaves no footprints, attacks people, portends death); Day 1967: 77, 84 (at bridge, glowing eyes, big as a calf, soundless tread, walks through walls); Harries 1968: 65–71 (accompanies cyclist, vanishes); Tongue 1970: 70–1 (attacks people; fictitious); Porter 1974: 89–92 (at bridge, invisible, attacks people); Barrett and Garrod 1976: 103–5 (howling, blow goes through, attacks people); Bunn 1977a (at bridge, at churchyard, at gate, glowing eyes, big as a calf, shaggy, with chain, invisible, headless, walks on hindlegs, blow goes through, explodes, vanishes, attacks people, throws people down, dangerous to touch, portends death); Bunn 1977b (howling, with chain); Bunn 1977c; Bord and Bord 1980: 86–7 (vanishes); Jennings 1994 (glowing eyes, big as a calf); Thompson 2000 (appears at midnight, glowing eyes, vanishes, portends misfortune); Westwood 2001 (runs a route, accompanies cyclist, glowing eyes, shaggy, with chain, invisible, visible to one only, headless, soundless tread, vanishes when run over, portends misfortune, portends death, saves from danger, 'guardian dog' tale type).

Northumberland: Walcott 1861: 309 (glowing eyes, portends death); 'Q' 1910–11: 391 (at bridge, in house, portends death, ghost of murder victim); Brown 1970 (saves from danger); Maloret 1987 (at churchyard, vanishes).

Nottinghamshire: Trubshaw 1994a: 9 (accompanies vehicle); Rice-Heaps 2002 (big as a calf, vanishes).

Oxfordshire: Jewitt 1903: 184 (glowing eyes); Briggs 1974: 97, 147.

Shropshire: Burne and Jackson 1883: 105 (glowing eyes, headless, vanishes, ghost of murder victim, ghost of suicide); Hayward 1938: 242 (invisible).

Somerset: Humphreys 1889: 243; Thornton 1897: 20–2 (at water, glowing eyes, explodes, vanishes, ghost of accident victim); Snell

1903: 257; Whistler 1908: 44 (attacks people, portends misfortune); Watson 1922 (glowing eyes); Mathews 1923: 68 (glowing eyes, visible to one only, vanishes, portends death); O'Donnell 1923: 20 (vanishes); O'Donnell 1934: 102; Tongue 1956 (glowing eyes, big as a calf; fictitious); Tongue 1965: 107–110 (at churchyard, at crossroads, in house, glowing eyes, explodes, ghost of suicide, portends death, 'guardian dog' tale type; all probably fictitious); Palmer 1973: 39, 126–9 (with chain, vanishes, portends death); Bord and Bord 1987: 47 (glowing eyes, shaggy, portends death).

Staffordshire: Bladen 1900–1: 142, 146–7 (at water, accompanies traveller, headless, ghost of suicide); Brighton 1937: 161, 175 (at water, big as a calf, blow goes through); Witcutt 1942: 126 (at water, ghost of murder victim); Haigh 1976 (invisible, vanishes); Raven 1978: 23 (glowing eyes, howling, portends death); Leese 1989: 23–9 (at churchyard, accompanies travellers, glowing eyes, invisible, sound of footsteps, walks through walls, vanishes, portends misfortune, portends death); Taylor 1995 (howling, portends misfortune).

Suffolk: Moor 1823: 142–3 (at water, big as a calf, attacks people); Forby 1830: 2.238 (big as a calf, throws people down); Emerson 1888 (glowing eyes, shaggy); James 1891: 32–4, 55 (in house, runs a route, glowing eyes, headless, soundless tread, attacks people); Gurdon 1895: 84–5, 91–2 (at gate, glowing eyes, big as a calf, shaggy, visible to one only, attacks people, throws people down, ghost of accident victim); Anderson and Hadow 1924: 353–4 (at gate, big as a calf, with chain, throws people down); Hood *et al* 1926: 369 (headless); Day 1954: 26 and 1958: 200–1 (at churchyard, appears at midnight); MacGregor 1955: 67–71 (runs a route, big as a calf, vanishes); Brown 1958: 179 (at churchyard); Day 1962: 640; Garner 1969: 182–3 (invisible, sound of footsteps); Porter 1974: 89 (glowing eyes, portends death); Bunn 1977a (at water, invisible, headless, blow goes through, vanishes, portends death); Boar and Blundell 1983: 76 (leaves no footprints, attacks people); Reeve 1988: 67–71 (at churchyard, appears at midnight, glowing eyes, big as a calf, walks through walls, leaves no footprints, vanishes, vanishes when run over, portends misfortune, portends death, saves from danger); Haining 1992: 44–5 (glowing eyes); Westwood 2001.

Surrey: Aitken 1950-1 (big as a calf).

Sussex: Lower 1861: 226; Geering 1884: 232–3 (runs a route, glowing eyes); Beckett 1909: 215–9 (walks through walls, portends misfortune, portends death); Hannah 1932: 157; O'Donnell 1948: 174 (in house, vanishes); Simpson 1973: 50 (headless); Wales 1992: 55, 94 (glowing eyes, big as a calf, howling); see also Staveley 2002.

Warwickshire: Bloom 1930: 100 (portends death); Palmer 1976: 79 (shaggy, portends death); Bird 1973: 49 (leaves no footprints); McGrory 1995 (glowing eyes, big as a calf, shaggy, walks through walls, explodes, dangerous to touch, portends death); Woodward 1988: 85; Turner 1993: 157 (vanishes).

Westmorland: Henderson 1879: 275–6 (at water, attacks people); Whiteside 1904: 350; Newman and Wilson 1952: 98–9 (appears at midnight, headless, portends death); Brown 1970: 8 (in house); Green 1973: 344 (in house, shaggy, vanishes); Lofthouse 1976: 39 and Findler 1979: 58 (runs a route, portends death); Findler 1979: 61–2 (appears at midnight, headless, portends death).

Wiltshire: Jefferies 1879: 110–1 (accompanies traveller); Olivier 1932: 75–6, 83 (in house, accompanies traveller); Brown 1958 (in house); Tongue 1970: 48–9 (glowing eyes, big as a calf, walks through walls, attacks people; fictitious); Wiltshire 1973: 1–16 (at water, appears at midnight, accompanies travellers, accompanies cyclist, glowing eyes, big as a calf, shaggy, with chain, visible to one only, headless, sound of footsteps, vanishes, vanishes when run over, throws people down, portends misfortune, portends death); Wiltshire 1984: 13–20 (in house, accompanies traveller, big as a calf, with chain, vanishes); Jordan 2000: 174–81 (at water, accompanies traveller, glowing eyes, vanishes).

Worcestershire: Bradley 1862: 297; Woodward 1866: 9 (at churchyard, appears at midnight, vanishes); Jenkins 1977: 177 (accompanies traveller, glowing eyes, soundless tread); Bord 1974: 7–8, reprinted in Bord 1980: 92–3 (in house, glowing eyes, vanishes); Turner 1993: 40–1 (appears at midnight, vanishes when run over); Spencer 2001: 275–6 (saves from danger).

Yorkshire: Hone 1827–8: 2.653–9, 775–83 and Dixon 1881: 251–7 (at bridge, accompanies traveller, glowing eyes, shaggy, with chain, invisible, vanishes, attacks people, portends death); Bramwell Brontë 1837 in Simpson 2003: 399 (with chain, portends death); Brontë 1847: chapter 12; Robinson 1862: 380 (at gate, accompanies travellers, howling, with chain, dangerous to touch, portends death); Atkinson 1868: 30 (glowing eyes, shaggy, howling, portends death); Robinson 1876: 11, 163 (at churchyard, glowing eyes, howling, soundless tread, portends death); Henderson 1879: 273–5 (at water, accompanies travellers, glowing eyes, big as a calf, shaggy, with chain, sound of footsteps, walks on hindlegs, blow goes through, vanishes, attacks people, dangerous to touch, portends death); Dawson 1882: 389; Lucas 1882 (glowing eyes, howling, with chain, portends death); Easther 1883: xxiii–iv, 96 (accompanies traveller, glowing eyes, big as a calf, visible to one only, sound of footsteps, vanishes, throws people down, portends death); MacQuoid 1883: 4 (glowing eyes, with chain); Cudworth 1886: 172 (accompanies traveller, glowing eyes, with chain, portends death); Parkinson 1888–9: 1.131–3 (at water, shaggy, with chain, soundless tread, vanishes); Nicholson 1890: 78 (glowing eyes, howling, portends death); Atkinson 1891a: 216 (runs a route, headless, vanishes); Atkinson 1891b: 150–1 (glowing eyes, shaggy); Baring-Gould 1892: 16–17 (glowing eyes, portends death); Morris 1892: 273 (glowing eyes, big as a calf); Hope 1893: 179–80 (at crossroads, at water, accompanies traveller, glowing eyes, big as a calf, shaggy, with chain, portends death); Gutch 1901 (glowing eyes, howling, portends death); Speight 1902: 158 (with chain, portends death); Bogg 1904: 245 (with chain); Fletcher 1912: 102–3 (accompanies traveller, big as a calf, glowing eyes, soundless tread); Southwart 1923: 26–8 (runs a route, glowing eyes, big as a calf); Hole 1940b: 154 (at bridge, headless, portends death); MacGregor 1955: 63–4 (glowing eyes, big as a calf, portends death); Mitchell 1969: 33, 39 and Briggs 1971: B1.15 ('guardian dog' tale type); Brown 1970 (howling, portends death); Mitchell 1973: 46; Lofthouse 1976: 44 (glowing eyes, big as a calf); Alexander 1978: 46–51 (vanishes); Salim 1983: 118 and Clarke and Wilson 1987: 43 (at crossroads, glowing eyes); Cunniff 1985: 29 (accompanies traveller); Pendleton 1986 (at churchyard, glowing eyes, shaggy, howling, portends death); Bord and Bord 1987: 45–6 (accompanies cyclist, glowing eyes, shaggy, blow goes through); Taylor 1990 (vanishes, portends death); Taylor 1991: 19 (vanishes); Linahan 1994: 35–9 (in house, accompanies cyclist, big as a calf, invisible, sound of footsteps, walks through walls, vanishes); Shepherd 1994: 45–6 (glowing eyes); Todd 2000 (glowing eyes, vanishes); Huddleston 2004 (accompanies vehicle).

Motifs

Black Dogs feature two or three times in Stith Thompson's great *Motif-Index of Folk Literature*, but the standard reference is E423.1.1. The list below contains only the most common features of their appearance.

Place and time of appearance

At bridge (16 instances in the list of *Local Traditions* above); see also Brown 1958: 182. The motif is E332.1 in general ghost lore – see Thompson 1955–8 for this and the following motif references.

At churchyard (22 instances); see also Brown 1958: 184, Woods 1959: 29 (legend-type 8), Bord and Bord 1980: 100–3. The motif is E333 in ghost lore.

At crossroads (6 instances); see also Bord and Bord 1980: 98.

At gate, or at a stile (11 instances); see also Bord and Bord 1980: 98, 101.

At water, which encompasses rivers, ditches, ponds and wells (27 instances); see also Brown 1958: 182, Woods 1959: 31 (legend-type 11), Bord and Bord 1980: 99–101. The nearest motif in ghost lore is E285 (ghost haunts well).

In house (27 instances); see also Woods 1959: 27 (legend-type 1). The motif is E338 in ghost lore.

Runs a route (24 instances); see also Woods 1959: 38 (legend-type 20), Bord and Bord 1980: 96. E272 is the general motif for road ghosts, but none is given for the kind of ghost that patrols a particular stretch of road.

Appears at midnight (17 instances); see also Woods 1959: 18 (motif A) and 66 (legend-type 100). The motif is E587.5 in ghost lore.

Behaviour

Accompanies traveller (35 instances); see also Woods 1959: 39 (legend-type 24). The motif is E332.2 in ghost lore.

Accompanies cyclist (9 instances).

Accompanies vehicle (9 instances).

Description

Glowing eyes (96 instances), Brown 1958: 181, Woods 1959: 18 (motif E) , Bord and Bord 1980: 79. The motif is E421.3 in ghost lore.

Big as a calf, or large as a donkey, or any other comparison of great size (62 instances); see also Bord and Bord 1980: 77.

Shaggy (31 instances); see also Brown 1958: 180, Bord and Bord 1980: 79.

Howling (24 instances); see also Bord and Bord 1980: 80. The motif is E402.2 in ghost lore.

With chain (30 instances); see also Brown 1958: 181, Bord and Bord 1980: 84. The nearest motif in ghost lore is E402.1.4 (invisible ghost rattles chain).

Invisible (19 instances); see also Bord and Bord 1980: 80. The motif is E421.1 in ghost lore.

Visible to one only (9 instances), Woods 1959: 18 (motif F). The motif is E421.1.1 in ghost lore.

Headless (31 instances); see also Brown 1958: 180–1, Bord and Bord 1980: 79. The motif is E422.1.1 in ghost lore.

Sound of footsteps, which is also implied in the names padfoot, trash, and gallytrot (16 instances); see also Bord and Bord 1980: 79. The motif is E402.1.2 in ghost lore.

Soundless tread (10 instances); see also Bord and Bord 1980: 80.

Walks on hindlegs (10 instances); see also Brown 1958: 181.

Blow goes through (18 instances); see also Bord and Bord 1980: 82–3.

Walks through walls (15 instances); see also Bord and Bord 1980: 86.

Leaves no footprints (6 instances); see also Bord and Bord 1980: 80. The motif is E421.2.1 in ghost lore.

Explodes (10 instances); see also Bord and Bord 1980: 87.

Vanishes (77 instances); see also Woods 1959: 18 (motif V), Bord and Bord 1980: 87. The motif is E407.2 in ghost lore.

Vanishes when run over, the Bluebell Hill motif (16 instances).

Interaction with people

Attacks people (22 instances); see also Woods 1959: 55 (legend-type 70). The motif is E261 in ghost lore.

Throws people down (10 instances).

Dangerous to touch (10 instances); see also Brown 1958: 187, Woods 1959: 45 (legend-type 36). The motif is E279.6 in ghost lore.

Portends misfortune (16 instances). The motif is E575 in ghost lore.

Portends death (68 instances). The motif is E574 in ghost lore.

Interpretation

Ghost of accident victim (5 instances); see also Brown 1958: 185 and Woods 1959: 30, 116 (legend-type 344), both of whom group all kinds of violent death together under one heading. The motif is E334.2.2 in ghost lore.

Ghost of murder victim (7 instances). The motif is E334.2.1 in ghost lore.

Ghost of suicide (5 instances); see also Woods 1959: 116 (legend-type 342). The motif is E334.4 in ghost lore.

Saves from danger (5 instances). The motif is E363 in ghost lore.

'Guardian dog' tale type (11 instances). This is really a migratory legend, but has no number as such; it appears as motif E363.2 (ac) in ghost lore.

Personal Experiences

1803 (reported), 'a servant at Durham' hears approaching shrieks and faints at the sound (Ritson 1831: 58).

1809, a scholar at Stoney Stanton (Leicestershire) hears a groaning sound before something like a shaggy dog rushes past him at bridge (Nichols 1795–1815: 4ii.970).

1810s, Catern Buckingham of North Hill (Cornwall) sees a dog which swells and explodes in fire when a broom is thrown at it (Spooner 1925–30a: 24–5).

1819, Robert Newton at Manchester is accompanied by a dog which suddenly appears to scare off two suspicious-looking men and then vanishes (Jackson 1855: 98).

1820, J.L. of Almondbury (Yorkshire) is accompanied on a journey by a dog which follows him home (Easther 1883: xxiii).

1825, Mr Drabble of Manchester has a dog place its paws on his shoulders and force him home (Hardwick 1872: 172).

1827 (reported), Billy Blakey of Grassington (Yorkshire) is accompanied by an invisible dog across the moors and then sees it lying on his doorstep (Hone 1827–8: 2.655–6 and Dixon 1881: 253–5).

1827 (reported), John Lambert at Skirethornes (Yorkshire) attacks a dog rather than give way to it, and is crushed to death (Hone 1827–8: 2.655–6 and Dixon 1881: 256–7).

1827 (reported), a stout, elderly man at Arncliffe (Yorkshire) goes to a cunning-woman, and is accompanied by a dog on the way home, shortly before his friend dies (Hone 1827–8: 2.775–83, may be fiction).

1847, Mary Stenner of Selworthy (Somerset) sees a dog run past her as far as a stream and then go up in a flash of fire (Thornton 1897: 20–2).

1848 (reported), a lady newly married in Cornwall sees a dog on her child's bed, unaware that it is a family death omen, and the child dies (Crowe 1848: 341).

1849 (reported), Mr Finch of Neatshead (Norfolk) kicks at a dog and his foot goes through it (Gunn 1849: 300).

1850s, Grace Blatchford and two friends at North Hill (Cornwall) are out walking when a dog passes between them (Spooner 1925–30a: 25).

1854 (reported), an old gentleman of Darlington (Durham) sees a dog, larger than a Newfoundland dog, staring at him in a lane (Longstaffe 1854: 13–14).

1856, a nurse from Lyme Regis(Devon/Dorset border), walking down Dog Lane, sees a dog which swells as she goes by, but her husband sees only mist (Chambers 1864: 2.434).

1862 (reported), a man from Leeds meets a dog by a stile and kicks it, on which it drags him across country to his own home (Robinson 1862: 380).

1864, James Woodward at Bordesley Abbey (Worcestershire), together with a friend, sees a dog for two successive nights while keeping watch in a ruined abbey (Woodward 1866: 95).

1864 (reported), a milkman of Aylesbury (Buckinghamshire) meets a dog which blocks the gate, and paralyses him when he hits it (Chambers 1864: 2.433).

1864 (reported), the village schoolmaster of Tring (Hertfordshire) has his path blocked by a dog when he is driving a cart past a gibbet (Chambers 1864: 2.433–4).

1865, Abe Mindham of Magdalen (Norfolk) is found dead of fright after seeing a dog approaching his cottage (Randell 1966: 99–100).

1866 (reported), Sally Dransfield of Swillington (Yorkshire) sees a dog rolling like a pack of wool on the ground before her and changing its shape (Henderson 1879: 273–4).

1866 (reported), a man in Horbury near Leeds sees a white dog and hits it but the blow goes through, it glares at him, and he runs home and dies (Henderson 1879: 274).

1866 (reported), a child at Wreghorn near Leeds sees a dog with flaming eyes leading a procession of howling dogs on the death of local squire (Henderson 1879: 275).

1870s, Mrs Jewell of St Giles-in-the-Wood (Devon), as a child, is accompanied by a dog when she is out walking with her father, and it vanishes (Day 1958: 212–3).

1870s, Mrs Smalley's grandfather from South Muskam (Nottinghamshire) is accompanied by a dog while driving his pony and trap (Trubshaw 1994a: 9).

1880 (reported), the coachman at Okehampton (Devon) and his passengers are accompanied by 'the black hound that haunts the moor' (Doe 1880: 100).

1880 (reported), a local man in Coventry hits a dog with his riding crop, when it explodes and throws him in ditch (McGrory 1995).

1880 (reported), a farmhand in Coventry sees a dog pass through a hedge and burst in a flash, shortly before his master's death (McGrory 1995).

1883 (reported), 'Adam' from Chipping (Lancashire) is accompanied by a dog on the way home (Bowker 1883: 27–36; this may derive from Wilkinson 1850).

1883 (reported), A.M. of Almondbury (Yorkshire) sees a dog change into a calf and follow him home, where he is unable to move or open the door (Easther 1883: xxiii).

1883 (reported), Jo B. of Almondbury (Yorkshire) is accompanied on his journey by a dog (Easther 1883: xxiv).

1884 (reported), the mother of Mrs. Dobbs at Alfriston (Sussex) sees a dog run down the field to look over a wall and then return (Geering 1884: 232–3).

1885 (reported), Johnnie Greenwood at Swancliffe near Ayscliffe (by which is probably meant Aycliffe, Co. Durham) is guarded from robbers who see a dog with him (Hare 1896–1900: 5.425).

1886, Mr Macgowan and a companion at Kidsgrove (Staffordshire) hear a dog rushing towards them, but can see nothing (Leese 1989: 23).

1886 (reported), a 'staunch Independent of the old school' at Bradford is followed by a dog when the owner of the Hall is dying (Cudworth 1886: 172).

1887, J. Blackmore of Washfield (Devon) kicks at a dog and nearly falls over when it vanishes (Chope 1928: 117–8).

1890s, a fishmonger at Godley Green (Cheshire) sees a yellow dog which walks backwards, and his blow goes through it (Hole 1937: 163).

1890s, a child at Godley Green (Cheshire) is accompanied by a yellow dog (Hole 1937: 163)

1890s, a lady staying at Godley Green (Cheshire) is followed by a yellow dog which vanishes (Hole 1937: 163).

1890s, Mrs Cooms' father at Great Durnford (Wiltshire) hits a dog and his blow goes through it (Wiltshire 1973: 12).

1890s, a young man at Leverton (Lincolnshire) is accompanied by a dog (Rudkin 1938: 113).

1890s, a cook at Church Stretton (Shropshire) sees a dog (Hayward 1938: 242).

1890s, a man from Hethersett (Norfolk) passes by a dog, which is whisked up by a gust of wind, and he sees its saucer eyes as it goes (Rye 1920: 28).

1891 (reported), 'a respectable old charwoman' of Geldeston (Norfolk) is walking with her daughter when a dog comes up behind them, but she only sees it when touched by the girl (James 1891: 9–11, Adams 1914: 187–92).

1891, 'the father of a servant of ours' at Aldeburgh (Suffolk) is attacked by a dog when he stops along an avenue of trees (James 1891: 33–4).

1892 (reported), a gentleman walking out late one night at Winchcombe (Gloucestershire) sees a man and dog walk through a closed gate (Turner 1993: 175–6).

1893, Thomas Jackson Reynard at Keighley (Yorkshire) is accompanied by a dog which protects him from robbers (Mitchell 1969: 33).

1893 (reported), a carter in Rockland (Norfolk) touches a dog with his cart and it bursts into flame (Bunn 1977a: 3–4).

1893 (reported), a lady from Great Yarmouth has a dog jump up and lean on her shoulders (Bunn 1977a: 4).

1893 (reported), a man from Gorleston (Norfolk) is thrown over a hedge when he insults a dog (Bunn 1977a: 4).

1893 (reported), 'one poor fellow' from Wakefield sees a dog walking beside him on the night his aunt dies (Hope 1893: 179–80).

1895, a miner from Diglake Colliery at Kidsgrove (Staffordshire) is accompanied back from the pit by a dog which vanishes, shortly before a mining disaster (Leese 1989: 24).

1895 (reported), a woman at Holmesfield (Derbyshire) is walking with a friend when one of them sees a dog and the other cannot, before a death (Addy 1895: 137).

1895 (reported), 'goodman Kemp' of Melton (Suffolk) sees a dog with a donkey's head and velvet hide on the toll-gate (Gurdon 1895: 91–2).

1896, Mr Barns of Leek (Staffordshire) meets a dog which growls and will not let him cross a bridge (Bladen 1900–1: 146).

1897, a man from Diss (Norfolk) sees a dog approaching a stile, and it vanishes (Bunn 1977a: 5).

1900s, drivers at Weymouth (Dorset) see a dog accompanying their trap along the road (Waring 1973: 3).

1900s, the monthly nurse from Kirton (Lincolnshire) sees a dog which speaks to her after she had said she was not frightened of it (Rudkin 1938: 116–7).

1900s, D.M. of Willoughton (Lincolnshire) is cycling when he sees a dog cross the road in front of him (Rudkin 1938: 125).

1900s, Mr and Mrs Reynolds of Southwold (Suffolk) see a dog when driving their cart, and it vanishes (MacGregor 1955: 70).

1900s, a woman from Swaby (Lincolnshire) is followed down to the bridge by a dog which vanishes (Miller 1984: 133).

1900 (reported), a traveller at Roborough Down (Devon) is accompanied by a dog which explodes at the crossroads (Hewett 1900: 39–41).

1900 (reported), M. Thelwall's grandfather in the Marshland of Norfolk is driving when a dog crosses the road in front of his terrified horse (Thelwall 1900–1: 297).

1902, William Thorne of Hoe Benham (Berkshire) sees a dog turn into a donkey walking on its hind legs (Miles 1907–8: 259).

1904 (reported), an old woman of Holden (Lancashire) is accompanied home after a night's card-playing by a dog which vanishes in a flash of fire (Wilkinson 1904–5: 4–5).

1910s, a boy in Norfolk is running an errand when he is interrupted by a dog, and he dies (Hole 1940a: 150).

1910s, Wilfred Turner of Quemerford (Wiltshire) sees a dog with a chain go through a closed door (Wiltshire 1973: 7).

1910s, a friend of Muriel Coburn's mother in Manton (Wiltshire) sees a dog with a chain in the house (Wiltshire 1973: 7).

1910s, Mrs L of Willoughton (Lincolnshire) is accompanied by a dog on outward and return journeys (Rudkin 1938: 126).

1910s, a man from Bradford (Devon) whistles to a dog to come and it makes an awful noise (Brown 1959: 40).

1910s, E.G. Pearse of Okehampton is riding a donkey down a lane when a dog appears and frightens him (St.Leger-Gordon 1965: 37, Brown 1982: 116).

1912, a boy of ten at Tockenham (Wiltshire) is frightened by a dog with a chain (Wiltshire 1984: 13–14).

1912, a woman from Barton (Lincolnshire) is accompanied home by a dog which frightens away an aggressive tramp before vanishing (Rudkin 1955: 390–1).

1912 (reported), a woman from Minchinhampton (Gloucestershire) is accompanied by dog which she can see through (Partridge 1912: 340).

1912 (reported), an old woman of Darrington (Yorkshire) is accompanied home by a dog each night in the dark months (Fletcher 1912: 102–3).

1914–18, Mrs Hallet of Chaffcombe (Somerset) sees a dog before her son is killed in World War I (Palmer 1973: 128).

1915, an old lady from Bridport (Dorset) sees a dog on the way back from church before her daughter's death (Waring 1966).

1915, Sidney Smalley of South Muskam (Nottinghamshire) often sees a dog while riding a motorbike, and once with his father (Trubshaw 1994a: 9).

1916 (reported), a man at the Hermitage, Ipstones (Staffordshire) kicks a dog and his foot goes through it (Brighton 1937: 175).

1917, Mrs M.F. Hall of Bungay (Suffolk) sees a dog run out of a gate and through the churchyard door (Reeves 1988: 70–1).

1920s, Mr Maslen of All Cannings (Wiltshire) is chased into the village by a dog (Wiltshire 1973: 13).

1920s, a fisherman from Kettleness (Yorkshire) sees a dog appear and vanish on several occasions (Alexander 1978: 47).

1920s, Mr E.F. Hext of Chagford (Devon) is accompanied when riding by a dog which cannot be touched (Brown 1982: 115).

1920s, Mrs A.M. Osborne of Tollesbury (Essex) is cycling when a dog accompanies her and blocks the road (Day 1969: 151–3).

1920s, Christopher Marlowe at Stiffkey (Norfolk) is pursued by a howling dog until he takes refuge in a cottage (Marlowe 1927: 198–204).

1920s, the librarian at Leek (Staffordshire) sees a dog walking behind her and her mother, and it vanishes (Haigh 1976).

1920s, the father of Mrs A.M. Wilson of Earsham (Suffolk) feels chill and sees a dog walk across the road and through a wall, leaving no footprints (Reeves 1988: 69–70).

1920s, J.K. of Caythorpe (Lincolnshire) is cycling beside a high stone wall when he is accompanied by a dog which vanishes (Miller 1984: 132).

1921, an acquaintance of Theo Brown at Cowling (Yorkshire) hears long shuddering cries (Brown 1970: 6).

1923 (reported), a lad of Stapley (Somerset) sees the dog before a family death but his sister, who was with him, sees nothing (Mathews 1923: 68).

1924 (reported), a member of Westleton WI (Suffolk) passes a dog at a stile (Anderson and Hadow 1924: 353–4).

1925 (reported), a van driver from Torrington (Devon) regularly sees a dog walking alongside his miller's waggon (Chope 1927: 161, Day 1958: 205–6).

1926, Ethel Rudkin at Dunwich abbey (Suffolk) sees a dog (Brown 1958: 179).

1926 (reported) 'Mr Furnass and I' at Blyth (Northumberland) see a dog appear at a cemetery, then spread out like a blanket and float away (Maloret 1987).

1927 (reported), the grandfather of an old sailor at Stiffkey (Norfolk) has his throat torn out by a dog (Marlowe 1927: 190).

1928, Mr Hooper of Chichester sees a dog run around his house, and it vanishes when cornered (O'Donnell 1948: 174).

1929 (reported), two women and a man from North Hill (Cornwall) are walking when they see a dog which pushes them aside, taking the crown of the road (Spooner 1925–30: 24).

1929, Ella Lambert of Halesworth (Suffolk) sees a dog the evening before a row of cottages burns down (Reeves 1988: 67).

1930s, Mrs Satterley is in a church near Chippenham where she sees a dog walking after a knight in armour (Brown 1958: 179 (Wiltshire 1973: 11).

1930s, Warren Armstrong at Chideock (Dorset), walking home with a friend, is accompanied by a dog which vanishes at the churchyard (Waring 1973: 5).

1930s, a man from Old Fletton (Cambridgeshire) sees a dog vanish into a pond (Bunn 1977a: 3).

1930s, 'witnesses' at Barnby (Suffolk) touch a dog and their hands go through it (Bunn 1977a: 5).

1930s, Mr Kent of Barham (Suffolk) hits a dog and the blow goes through it (Bunn 1977a: 5).

1930s, a courting couple from Ab Kettleby (Leicestershire) see a dog before the death of the woman's father (Bell 1992: 5).

1930s, Mr E. Ramsey of Bawburgh (Norfolk) is cycling when he stops because there is a dog in front of him, and this saves him from an oncoming car (Reeve 1988: 67–8, Westwood 2001: 101–2).

1930, Greta Shirt of Upper Booth (Derbyshire) sees a dog pass through a wire fence (MacGregor 1955: 162–3).

1930, a man from Buxton Lamas (Norfolk) sees a dog appear and vanish before a death (Bunn 1977a: 4).

1930 (reported), Charles Walton of Alveston (Warwickshire) meets a dog on way home for nine evenings, and a headless lady on the tenth, after which his sister dies (Bloom 1930: 100).

1930 (reported), a man of North Hill (Cornwall) sees a dog on the way to a bridge, but it vanishes when he gets a stick ready (Spooner 1925–30b: 26).

1930 (reported), George White of Lewannick (Cornwall) is thrown aside onto a stoneheap when he tries to obstruct a dog (Spooner 1925–30b: 26–7).

1930 (reported), a woman and a man at Linkinhorne (Cornwall) are driving home when they see a dog jump into road and vanish (Spooner 1930b: 27).

1931, Mr H. Holmes of Barton Quarry (Yorkshire) is out cycling when he sees a stream of dogs which cannot be touched running past him (Bord and Bord 1987: 45–6).

1931 (reported), a lad from Down St Mary (Devon) sees a dog running past the schoolhouse and then hears the crash of falling masonry (Day 1958: 209).

1931 (reported), Mrs Jewell of Great Torrington (Devon) is out riding when a dog appears and makes her pony shy (Day 1958: 213).

1932, Constance Drummond at Frithelstock (Devon) thinks she has run over a dog on a narrow road by cliffs, but finds it has vanished (Day 1958: 214–6).

1930 (reported), a man at Wilbury (Wiltshire) is accompanied by a dog while walking (Olivier 1932: 75–6).

1933, Mr M. of Willoughton (Lincolnshire) is pushed against a post by an invisible dog (Rudkin 1938: 123).

1933, Mr L.L. of West Halton (Lincolnshire) is cycling when a dog appears beside him, keeping pace with him however fast he rides (Miller 1984: 132).

1934, an Irish labourer at Willoughton (Lincolnshire) is accompanied on the road by a dog (Rudkin 1938: 126).

1934 (reported), Mr Barker at Eresby (Lincolnshire) is riding with a woman passenger as pillion when they both see a white dog (Welby 1934–5: 132–3).

1935, a farmer's wife at Kirton (Lincolnshire) sees a dog come into her house and walk around the kitchen (Rudkin 1938: 116).

1935, H.B. of Manston (Lincolnshire) sees a dog lying by the roadside on a culvert (Miller 1984: 133).

1935 (reported), Mrs R. of Newton St Cyres (Devon) sees a dog walking on its hindlegs through the room where a girl was murdered (Chope 1936: 87–8).

1936, Hugh Braun at Foxham (Wiltshire) sees a dog which vanishes when he runs it over, and misfortune follows (Wiltshire 1973: 6).

1936 (reported), 'the genial schoolmistress from Manton' (Lincolnshire) is cycling when a dog runs alongside her (Rudkin 1938: 114–6).

1937 (reported), Mr C. at Willoughby (Lincolnshire), a Methodist preacher, is accompanied by a dog through a wood (Rudkin 1938: 122–3).

1937, the father of R.B. from Burton Stather (Lincolnshire) sees a dog run alongside him as he cycles home (Miller 1984: 132–3).

1937, motorists on the A6 over Shap (Cumberland) see a dog racing in front of their cars and then leaping over a stone wall to a sheer drop (Findler 1979: 58).

1938, Ernest Whiteland of Ditchingham (Norfolk) sees a dog come towards him and vanish (MacGregor 1955: 66–7).

1938 (reported), Mrs B. of Algarkirk (Lincolnshire) sees a dog run out from under some trees (Rudkin 1938: 113).

1938 (reported), a friend of Mrs M. and his sister at Kesteven (Lincolnshire) are accompanied by a dog when walking through a wood (Rudkin 1938: 113).

1938 (reported), Mrs P. of West Stockwith (Lincolnshire) sees a dog go into the house (Rudkin 1938: 114).

1938 (reported), the mother of Mrs D. from Crosby (Lincolnshire) is guarded from unpleasant characters by a dog which vanishes (Rudkin 1938: 117).

1938 (reported), 'a hardworking young woman' from South Kelsey (Lincolnshire) sees a dog walk along and then vanish (Rudkin 1938: 117–8).

1938 (reported), 'a hard-headed man' from Willoughton (Lincolnshire) hears a dog push through the hedge with a crackling sound (Rudkin 1938: 122, 123

1938 (reported), the father of J.B. at Willoughton (Lincolnshire) sees a dog vanish with a sudden crack by a tree on the bend of a road (Rudkin 1938: 124).

1938 (reported), Mrs G.B. of Grayingham (Lincolnshire) hits a dog with her umbrella but the blow goes through it (Rudkin 1938: 125).

1938 (reported), Grace Smith's grandmother and her children at Lymington (Hampshire) are at home when they see a dog run across the room and vanish (Smith 1938).

1938 (reported), a family farming at Stewkley (Buckinghamshire) often see a dog running beside their dog-cart, and then it vanishes (Tebbult 1945).

1938 (reported), Mr Powell of Manningtree (Essex) sees a dog running down the hill, shortly before a death (Newman and Wilson 1952: 100).

1939, Jimmy Farman of St Olaves (Suffolk) sees a dog with eyes like railway lamps, which terrifies his own dog (Haining 1992: 44–5).

1939, William Nott is driving a bus at Blackmoor Gate (Devon) when he sees a dog and some sheep on the road ahead, but when he runs them over, there is nothing there (Farson 1978: 30, Beer 1984: 32, Brown 1985: 241–2, Brown 1988: 229).

1939, Mr C.W. Hopwood of Kidsgrove (Staffordshire) is accompanied by a dog which frightens him (Leese 1989: 25).

1940s, a girl aged four at Bredon (Worcestershire) is in bed when she sees a dog enter the room (Bord 1974: 7–8, reprinted in Bord 1980: 92–3).

1940s, the tenants of a house at Snitterfield (Warwickshire) see a dog run over their garden without leaving footprints (Bird 1973: 49).

1940s, 'a very frightened Women's Institute member' from Cricklade (Wiltshire) sees a dog (Wiltshire 1973: 4).

1940s, a farmer and a Land Girl at Pewsey (Wiltshire) both see a dog led by a lady in black (Wiltshire 1973: 16).

1940s, an American serviceman stationed at Walberswick (Suffolk) sees and hears a dog attacking his house throughout the night, but there is no trace of it in the morning (Boar and Blundell 1983: 76).

1940s, a woman from Ab Kettleby (Leicestershire) sees a dog snarling at her before her husband is killed in action (Bell 1992: 5).

1940s, Councillor Turner from Kidsgrove (Staffordshire) hears the sound of a large animal panting and running hard by him (Leese 1989: 24).

1940, a cyclist at Scawby (Lincolnshire) is riding when a dog crosses the road in front of him (Miller 1984: 133).

1943, Stephen Jenkins at Bewdley (Worcestershire) sees a dog trot by him on the road (Jenkins 1977: 177).

1944, a woman from Winfarthing (Norfolk) sees a dog approach the house before a death (Bunn 1977a: 4).

1945, John Harries at East Dereham (Norfolk) is cycling when he is followed by a dog which vanishes (Harries 1968: 70–1).

1945, a man at Hilgay (Norfolk) hears frightening, ear-splitting baying but sees nothing (Bunn 1977c: 4).

1945, Nurse A. Wrigley at Kidsgrove (Staffordshire) sees a light-coloured tall dog following her before a local fire (Leese 1989: 28–9).

1946, William Fell from Wigborough (Essex) is driving a cart when a dog accompanies him (Day 1954: 30, 1958: 201, 1962: 641 and 1973: 11–12).

1947, a man at Chilham (Kent) sees a dog lope across the track behind a barrow (Bord and Bord 1987: 49).

1949, a waterworker at Coventry passes an enormous dog in a field (McGrory 1995).

1950s, a man from Donhead St Mary (Wiltshire) sees a dog (Wiltshire 1973: 9).

1950s, a Midland schoolmaster on holiday at Kettleness (Yorkshire) sees a dog which appears from the sea and looks evil (Alexander 1978: 48).

1950s, C.E. of Swaby (Lincolnshire) is walking when she hears the scuffling of feet all around her (Miller 1984: 133).

1950s, Mrs M.F. Hall of Bungay (Suffolk) sees a dog run across the street and disappear near the allotments (Reeves 1988: 71).

1950 (reported), Miss Baker's grandmother at Little Downham (Cambridgeshire) sees a dog and never gets over the fright (Oates and Wood 1998: 59).

1951 (reported), PC Stonehouse at Mow Cop (Staffordshire) sees a dog run through the iron gates of the churchyard (Leese 1989: 25).

1953, a man from Manningtree (Essex) sees a dog (MacGregor 1955: 72).

1954 (reported), 'Fred's sister' from Spinney, Cambridgeshire sees a dog glaring at her, and runs (Day 1954: 25).

1954 (reported), Lady Walsingham and Lady Rendlesham at Leiston (Suffolk) wait up in the churchyard and see a dog leave it at midnight (Day 1954: 26 and 1958: 200–1).

1954 (reported), Mr Wilson of Hempnall (Norfolk) is cycling when a dog crosses the road in front of him and vanishes (Day 1954: 28).

1954 (reported), 'the lady of the old family' at Leeds Castle (Kent) sees a dog which appears before a disaster and acts as a warning (Day 1954: 32–3).

1955 (reported), an old man at Wharfedale (Yorkshire) sees a dog (MacGregor 1955: 63).

1955 (reported), a woman and her sister-in-law from Walberswick (Suffolk) see a dog (MacGregor 1955: 68–9).

1955 (reported), an old lady from Stevenage (Hertfordshire) sees a large curly-haired dog (Oates and Wood 1998: 39).

1956 (reported), 'a small blind boy' at Thetford (Norfolk) feels a dog trying to push him into water (Porter 1974: 89).

1957, an old lady from Beaminster (Dorset) is at home when a dog walks round her chair shortly before her death (Waring 1966).

1958, an old lady from Hockley (Essex) is accompanied to the bus stop by a dog (Maple 1964: 186).

1958 (reported), a man at Hatfield Peverell (Essex) is driving a cart when he sees a dog and strikes out at it, it explodes and burns the cart (Brown 1958: 187).

1959, a family at Uplyme (Dorset/Devon border) see a dog float across the road (Brown 1982: 119).

1960s, a man at Sheringham (Norfolk) is cycling when he is accompanied by a dog with its chain clinking on the ground (Westwood 2001: 111).

1960s, Ashley Scully at Wentworth (Yorkshire) is cycling when a dog runs alongside him and then through him (Linahan 1994: 35–6).

1960 (reported), Mrs Garth-Heyworth of Crosscombe (Cornwall) sees a dog run into the house and upstairs, where it vanishes (Brown 1962: 27–8).

1962 (reported), Tom Stirling of Salthouse (Norfolk) sees a dog pass through a closed gate (Day 1962: 640).

1962 (reported), Leslie Goodwin of Walberswick (Suffolk) meets a dog in the lane (Day 1962: 640).

1962 (reported), Robert Norgate and Agnes Abel at Coltishall (Norfolk) hear a dog pass them on the bridge (Day 1962: 640, Day 1967: 84).

1963 (reported), Mrs Rideout of Woodcutts (Dorset) is at home when an earless black greyhound runs across the room (Parke 1963: 486).

1963 (reported), Miss Williams' grandfather at Woodyates (Dorset) sees a dog on his cart, which vanishes when he sticks a pitchfork through it (Parke 1963: 486).

1965, Mr Pease of Hockley (Essex) sees a dog appear and vanishes before a family death (Bunn 1977a: 4 and Bunn 1981: 11).

1967, Mr F. Dineen at Ingrave (Essex) sees a brown dog with fiery eyes on the road before deaths in the family (Bunn 1981: 11).

1967 (reported), a young farmer from Sheringham (Norfolk) sees a dog cross the road and pass through a gate (Day 1967: 84).

1968, a man from Barnby (Norfolk) sees a dog with a chain (Westwood 2001).

1969, a motorist at Okehampton (Devon) drives through a dog, which vanishes (Clark 1993: 400).

1969 (reported), the stepfather of Chris Merritt at Hilmarton (Wiltshire) is thrown off his bicycle by something dragging a chain (Wiltshire 1973: 8).

1969 (reported), John Harrison from Ramsbury (Wiltshire) hears an invisible dog rattling a chain (Wiltshire 1973: 13).

1969 (reported), a friend of Alan Garner in Suffolk hears the footsteps of a dog pass him on the road (Garner 1969: 182–3).

1970s, a man from Butley (Essex) is pushing his bicycle uphill, when a dog runs downhill through him and the bicycle (Jennings 1994).

1970, Mrs M. Whitehead of Bungay (Suffolk) sees a dog run past her when her sister dies (Reeves 1988: 70).

1970 (reported), Mrs Read's grandfather at Horton (Wiltshire) is accompanied by a dog with blazing eyes before his grandfather's death (Wiltshire 1973: 5).

1970 (reported), 'a Burbage WI member's father' from Grafton (Wiltshire) is walking when he sees a dog, but a friend sees nothing (Wiltshire 1973: 10).

1971, a couple at Stert (Wiltshire) see a dog passes their pony cart and vanish (Wiltshire 1973: 15).

1971 (reported), a man from Cromer (Norfolk) hits a dog, and his stick goes through it (Bunn 1977a: 5–6).

1972, Cecil Williamson at Buckfastleigh (Devon) is visiting the churchyard when he meets with a dog, which is substantial at first, and then his hands go through it (Williamson 1995).

1972, Graham Grant at Gorleston (Norfolk) sees a dog at a distance before it vanishes (Bord and Bord 1980: 86–7).

1972 'Tom Morgan' from Dartmoor sees a dog in his house which explodes when struck with a poker, damaging windows and roof (Innes 1983a).

1973, a worker on a pipeline at Blythburgh (Suffolk) hears the sound of an invisible dog before a death in the family (Bunn 1977a: 6).

1973 (reported), a man in Lincolnshire is accompanied by a dog which vanishes (Wiltshire 1984: 18).

1973 (reported), Clarence Daniel's mother at Calver (Derbyshire) is accompanied along a lonely stretch of road by a dog which passes through a wall (Daniel 1973: 44).

1973 (reported), a Methodist minister at Stoney Middleton (Derbyshire) is protected from unsavoury characters by a guardian dog (Daniel 1973: 44–5).

1974 (reported), Mrs Coles of Wootton Rivers (Wiltshire) is driving when she sees two dogs in the road (Wiltshire 1984: 14).

1974 (reported), a man from Melksham is chased along the road by a dog or bear (Wiltshire 1984: 15).

1974 (reported), Dick Grey of Longleat sees a dog (Wiltshire 1984: 15).

1974 (reported), a man from Clopton (Suffolk) sees a thing with eyes appear and announce a death (Porter 1974: 89).

1976 (reported), a retired builder from Minchinhampton (Gloucestershire) sees a headless dog (Farson 1978: 31).

1976, a man from Wrawby (Lincolnshire) has a dog leap on him while he sleeps (Miller 1984: 134).

1976 (reported), Jean Haigh's grandfather from Leek (Staffordshire) comes home in shock after meeting a dog (Haigh 1976).

1976 (reported), Sam Rudd of Salthouse (Norfolk) is pursued back home by a howling dog, and bullets pass through it (Barrett and Garrod 1976: 103–5).

1976 (reported), Jessica Lofthouse's great-great-grandfather at Greenhow Hill (Yorkshire) often sees a dog on the road (Lofthouse 1976: 44).

1977, a woman driving at Ulceby (Lincolnshire) brakes to avoid colliding with a dog which vanishes (Miller 1984: 134).

1978, a married couple driving at Exford (Somerset) see a dog with dirty white hair staring balefully at their car before a death (Bord and Bord 1987: 47).

1978 (reported), 'the grandfather of a local farmer' at Liverton (Devon) is driving a cart when he sees a dog walking on its hindlegs alongside the hedge (Brown 1978a: 217).

1980s, a group of schoolfriends at Accrington (Lancashire) see a dog running around the area of a disused power station (Jeffrey 2004).

1981, a man from Luton (Bedfordshire) sees a dog (Rickard 1981: 45).

1982, Maurice Knowles of Lydford (Devon) sees a curious eyeless pig-snouted dog in his field (Rickard 1983: 53–5).

1982, Mrs Crane of Bacton (Norfolk) drives past a dog with one glowing eye (Jennings 1994).

1982 (reported), a woman from Okehampton (Devon) is in a wood when a dog appears to protect her (Brown 1982: 114).

1983, a woman from Barrow on Humber (Lincolnshire) is driving when a dog glides across the road ahead of her car (Miller 1984: 134).

1984, Mr Lee of Molland (Devon) brakes his car as a huge dog runs towards him and vanishes (Beer 1984: 33).

1984 (reported), Mr Nutley of Burbage (Wiltshire) is accompanied by a dog which vanishes (Wiltshire 1984: 14).

1984 (reported), Kathleen Wiltshire at Wootton Rivers (Wiltshire) is walking when a huge dog passes her and her own dog (Wiltshire 1984: 20).

1985 (reported), a night cook at Pontefract Infirmary is accompanied home from work by a dog, whichever way she goes (Cunniff 1985: 29).

1986, 'Mrs X' of Hull and members of her family see a two-dimensional dog which vanishes, shortly before a death (Taylor 1990).

1986, Helen Woodley at Little Cowarne (Herefordshire) sees a dog walk across a lane by the church and vanish (Woodley 1994: 33).

1986, Robert Harman of South Tuckswood (Suffolk) hears scratching in the yard and sees a huge dog with red eyes which leaps over the wall (Reeves 1988: 68–9).

1988 (reported), a man from Lowestoft (Suffolk) sees a dog before a fishing vessel sinks with all crew (Reeves 1988: 67).

1989, 'a trio of 17-year-old boys', Buckhurst Hill (Essex) see a dog in a graveyard, also seen by a motorist, and it vanishes when he runs it over (Goss 1992a: 201, Goss 1992b).

1990s, Christine Bright of Warminster (Wiltshire) sees a dog cross the road ahead of her car (Jordan 2000: 177).

1991, Victoria Rice-Heaps of Worksop (Nottinghamshire) sees a dog cross the road ahead of her car (Rice-Heaps 2002).

1991 (reported), a friend of Ian Taylor driving between Whitby and Pickering (Yorkshire) sees a large dog, sitting on a barrow, which melts away (Taylor 1991: 19).

1992 (reported), Edwin Bennett from the western part of the Isle of Wight is driving when he collides with a dog which vanishes (Baldwin 1992: 17–18).

1993, Terry and Marie Veale of South Wraxall (Wiltshire) see a dog cross their path and vanish (Jordan 2000: 180–1).

1993, Alec Fox of North Anston (Yorkshire) encounters a dog when climbing a rock outcrop (Linahan 1994: 6–7).

1993 (reported), a lady out walking on Brewery Hill (Warwickshire) sees a dog fade out and rise into the air (Turner 1993: 156).

1994 (reported) a bridal couple lodging at Mosborough Hall (Yorkshire) see a dog rest its head on their bed and then vanish (Linahan 1994: 38).

1994 (reported), the Strong family of Dinnington (Yorkshire) hear an invisible dog scratching at their back door (Linahan 1994: 38–9).

1995, James Sanderson and three friends driving home from Smarden (Kent) stop in fog and see a dog as big as the car walk past (Tudor 2004).

1995 (reported), a man from Devizes (Wiltshire) sees a dog cross his path and vanish (Jordan 2000: 178).

1996, Mr G.E. Thompson of Hemby (Norfolk) sees a fierce dog in the road (Thompson 2000).

1996, 'two paranormal investigators' in the city centre of Manchester run over a dog which vanishes (Billingsley 1997).

1998 (reported), a young soldier at Bradshaw (Lancashire) sees a dog which leaps into the air and vanishes when touched (Fields 1998: 38).

1999, Graham and Stevie of Billingham (Yorkshire) repeatedly see a dog with glowing eyes (Todd 2000).

2000 (reported), Frances Price and Lois Holland of Totteridge (Wiltshire) are out walking when a dog passes them (Jordan 2000: 180).

2000 (reported), Margaret Bellhouse from Tunstead Milton (Derbyshire) sees a dog walk downhill behind her and vanish (Clarke 1991: 76 and Clarke 2000: 60).

2000 (reported), 'Granny' from Tunstead Milton (Derbyshire) is accompanied home by a guardian dog (Clarke 2000: 91).

2001 (reported), two men from Flegg (Norfolk) are out walking when a dog is seen by only one of them, and he dies (Westwood 2001: 107).

2002, Martin Jeffrey and his partner in Manchester see a dog walk through the walls of a building (Jeffrey 2004).

2004 (reported), N.H. Huddleston's grandfather in Wharfedale is accompanied on his rounds as a commercial traveller by a dog, which opens the gates (Huddleston 2004).

2004 (reported), 'Wiccawillow' in Cambridgeshire sees a dog with a hard looking face the night before her father dies.

References

anon., 1642, *Observations upon Prince Rupert's White Dog, called Boy*, London, T.B.

anon., 1643, *A Dialogue between Prince Rupert's Dogge, whose name is Pvddle ...*, London, I. Smith

anon., 1644, *A Dog's Elegy or Rupert's Tears*, London; G.B.

anon., 1638, *The Discovery of a London Monster, called The Blacke Dogge of New-gate.* London, M.P. for Robert Wilson.

Ackroyd, Peter, 2000, *London: The biography*, Chatto and Windus.

Adams, Morley, 1914, *In the Footsteps of Borrow and Fitzgerald*, Jarrow and Sons.

Addy, Sidney Oldall, 1895, *Household Tales and Traditional Remains: Collected in the counties of York, Lincoln, Derby and Nottingham*, David Nutt.

Aitken, Barbara, 1950-1, 'Bullbeggar Lane, Horsell, Surrey', *Folk-lore* 61/2, 463.

Alexander, Marc, 1978, *To Anger the Devil*, Neville Spearman.

Alvarado, C. S., 2000, 'Out-of-body experiences', in E. Cardeña, S. J. Lynn, and S. Krippner (eds.), *Varieties of Anomalous Experience: Examining the scientific evidence*, APA.

American Sleep Disorders Association (ASDA), *International Classification of Sleep Disorders: Diagnostic and coding manual (ICSD)*, ASDA.

Anderson, Ruth, and Grace E. Hadow, 1924, 'Scraps of English folklore: IX', *Folk-Lore* 35, 346–60.

Arnold, Neil, 2003, 'Kent's phantom hounds'; downloaded July 2004 from www.yourcounty.co.uk/Kent51/kentblackdogs.html.

Atkinson, John, 1868, *A Glossary of the Cleveland Dialect*, John Russell Smith.

Atkinson, John, 1891a, *Forty Years in a Moorland Parish*, Macmillan.

Atkinson, John, 1891b, *The Last of the Giant Killers: Or, the exploits of Sir Jack of Danby Dale*, Macmillan.

Aylott, Muriel, 1969, 'The Quaker Oat Man, black magic, cheese, headless dogs, farming, haunting and the headless men', *Dorset* 7, 16–17.

Baldick, Julian, 2000, *Animal and Shaman: Ancient religions of Central Asia,* I B Taurus.
Baldwin, Gay, 1992, *More Ghosts of the Isle of Wight,* Gay Baldwin.
Baldwin-Ives, Matthew, 1991, 'Black Dogs and boggards', *Markstone* 5, 18–19 and 7, 24.
Barham, Tony, 1973, *Witchcraft in the Thames Valley,* Spurbooks.
Baring-Gould, Sabine, 1892, *Strange Survivals,* Methuen.
Barkley, C.W., 1872, 'Mauthe dog', *Notes and Queries* 4 ser. 10, 217.
Barnes, William, 1962, *The Poems of William Barnes,* ed. Bernard Jones, Southern Illinois UP.
Barrett, Vera, *et al*, 1985, *A History of Melbury Abbas,* Barrett.
Barrett, W.H., and R.P. Garrod, 1976, *East Anglian Folklore and Other Tales,* Routledge and Kegan Paul.
Bayless, R., 1973, *Apparitions and Survival of Death,* University Books.
Beckett, Arthur, 1909, *The Spirit of the Downs,* Methuen.
Beddington, Winifred G., and Elsa B. Christy (eds), 1937, *It Happened in Hampshire,* Hampshire Federation of Women's Institutes.
Beer, Trevor, 1984, *The Beast of Exmoor: Fact or legend?,* Countryside Publications.
Bell, David, 1992, *Leicestershire and Rutland Ghosts and Legends,* Countryside Books.
Billingsley, John, 1997, 'Black Dog', *Northern Earth,* 69, 4.
Bird, Vivian, 1973, *Warwickshire,* Batsford.
Blacker, Carmen, 2001, 'Theo Brown (1914–1993)', in H.E. Davidson and A. Chaudhri, (eds), *Supernatural Enemies,* Carolina Academic Press.
Bladen, W. Wells, 1900–1, 'Folklore of North Staffordshire, chiefly collected at Stone', *Tr. of the North Staffordshire Field Club* 35, 133–85.
Bloom, J. Harvey, 1930, *Folk Lore, Old Customs and Superstitions in Shakespeare Land,* Mitchell Hughes and Clarke.
Boar, Roger, and Nigel Blundell, 1983, *The World's Greatest Ghosts,* Octopus.
Bogg, Edmund, 1904, *Lower Wharfedale: The old city of York and the Ainsty,* John Heywood.

Bogoras, Waldemar, 1904, *The Chukchee,* New York.
Bond, Lillian, 1956, *Tyneham, a Lost Heritage,* Longmans.
Bord, Janet, 1974, 'Some Fortean ramblings', *Fortean Times* 7, 6–8.
Bord, Janet and Colin Bord, 1980, *Alien Animals: A worldwide investigation*, Granada.
Bord, Janet, and Colin Bord, 1987, *Modern Mysteries of Britain,* Grafton.
Bosley, Keith (trans.), 1989, *The Kalevala: An epic poem after oral tradition by Elias Lönnrot.* Oxford UP.
Bowker, James, 1883, *Goblin Tales of Lancashire,* Swan Sonnenschein.
Bradley, Edward (as Cuthbert Bede), 1862, *The Curate of Cranston and Other Stories,* Saunders, Otley and Co.
Brand, John, 1777, *Observations on Popular Antiquities: Including the whole of Mr. Bourne's* Antiquitates Vulgares, T. Saint.
Brand, John, 1849, *Observations on the Popular Antiquities of Great Britain,* ed. Henry Ellis, Henry G. Bohn.
Brandon, S.G.F., 1967, *The Judgement of the Dead: An historical and comparative study of the idea of a* post-mortem *judgement in the major religions,* Weidenfeld and Nicholson.
Braude, S. E., 1991. 'Apparitions', in S. E. Braude, *The Limits of Influence: Psychokinesis and the philosophy of science,* Routledge.
Braude, S. E., 2003, *Immortal Remains: The evidence for life after death,* Rowman and Littlefield.
Bray, Anna, 1838, *Traditions, Legends, Superstitions and Sketches of Devonshire,* John Murray.
Briggs, Katharine M., 1971, *A Dictionary of British Folk-Tales in the English Language,* Routledge and Kegan Paul.
Briggs, Katharine M., 1974, *The Folklore of the Cotswolds,* Batsford.
Brighton, Fred, 1937, *The Tale of Ipstones,* E. Blocksidge.
Brockie, William, 1886, *Legends and Superstitions of the County of Durham,* B. Williams.
Brontë, Charlotte (as Currer Bell), 1847, *Jane Eyre,* Smith Elder and Co.
Brooks, John Attwood, 1994, *The Good Ghost Guide,* Jarrold.
Brown, Theo, 1955, '52nd report on folklore', *Tr. of the Devonshire Assoc.,* 87, 353–9.
Brown, Theo, 1958, 'The Black Dog', *Folk-lore,* 69, 175–192.
Brown, Theo, 1959, 'The Black Dog in Devon', *Tr. of the Devonshire Assoc.* 91, 38–44.
Brown, Theo, 1962, 'Living images', *Folklore,* 73, 25–40.

Brown, Theo, 1964, '61st report on folklore', *Tr. of the Devonshire Assoc.,* 96, 95–9.

Brown, Theo, 1970, 'The Black Dog in the North Country', *Lore and Language,* 1ii, 6–8

Brown, Theo, 1978a, '75th report on folklore', *Tr. of the Devonshire Assoc.,* 110, 214–8.

Brown, Theo, 1978b, 'The Black Dog in English folklore', in J.R. Porter and W.M.S. Russell (eds), *Animals in Folklore,* Folklore Society.

Brown, Theo, 1979, *The Fate of the Dead,* Mistletoe Series 12, Folklore Society.

Brown, Theo, 1982, *Devon Ghosts,* Jarrold.

Brown, Theo, 1983, '80th report on folklore', *Tr. of the Devonshire Assoc.,* 115, 171–5

Brown, Theo, 1985, '82nd report on folklore', *Tr. of the Devonshire Assoc.,* 117, 240–2.

Brown, Theo, 1988, '85th report on folklore', *Tr. of the Devonshire Assoc.,* 120, 227–30.

Bunn, Ivan, 1976, 'Black Dogs and water', *Fortean Times* 17, 12–13.

Bunn, Ivan, 1977a, 'Black Shuck: I', *Lantern,* 18, 3–6.

Bunn, Ivan, 1977b, 'Black Shuck: II', *Lantern,* 19, 4–8.

Bunn, Ivan, 1977c, 'Black Shuck: III', *Lantern,* 20, 2–3.

Bunn, Ivan, 1981, 'Phantom dogs in Essex', *Essex Landscape Mysteries,* 3, 10–12.

Burne, Charlotte Sophia, and Georgina F. Jackson, 1883, *Shropshire Folk-Lore: A sheaf of gleanings,* Trübner.

Carpenter, Thomas H., 1991, *Art and Myth in Ancient Greece,* Thames and Hudson.

Chambers, Robert, 1864, *The Book of Days,* W. and R. Chambers.

Choice Notes from 'Notes and Queries': Folk Lore, 1859, Bell and Daldy.

Chope, R. Pearse, 1927, 'Twenty-eighth report on Devonshire folk-lore', *Tr. of the Devonshire Assoc.,* 59, 147–72.

Chope, R. Pearse, 1928, 'Twenty-ninth report on Devonshire folk-lore', *Tr. of the Devonshire Assoc.,* 60, 111–34.

Chope, R. Pearse, 1936, 'Thirty-sixth report on Devonshire folk-lore', *Tr. of the Devonshire Assoc.,* 68, 81–98.

Chorvinsky, Mark, 1989, 'Our strange world', *Fate,* (Sept), 39–41.

Clark, Jerome, 1993, *Unexplained! 347 strange sightings, incredible occurrences, and puzzling physical phenomena,* Visible Ink.

Clark, W.G., 1926, *In Breckland Wilds,* R. Scott.

Clarke, David, 1991, *Ghosts and Legends of the Peak District*, Jarrold.
Clarke, David, 2000, *Supernatural Peak District*, Robert Hale.
Clarke, David, and Rob Wilson, 1987, *Strange Sheffield: Legend, folklore and legends of Hallamshire*, ASSAP.
Cockayne, O. (ed.), 1866, *Seinte Marharete*, EETS, London.
Conesa, J., 1995, 'Relationship between isolated sleep paralysis and geomagnetic influences: a case study', *Perceptual and Motor Skills*, 80, 1263–73.
Conesa, J., 1997, 'Isolated sleep paralysis, vivid dreams and geomagnetic influences: II', *Perceptual and Motor Skills*, 85, 579–84.
Cook, C. M., and M.A. Persinger, 1997, 'Experimental induction of the "sensed presence" in normal subjects and an exceptional subject', *Perceptual and Motor Skills*, 85, 683–93.
Coxe, A.D.H., 1975, *Haunted Britain*, Pan.
Cranworth, Emily Francis, 1900–1, 'East Anglian superstitions: II', *Eastern Counties Magazine*, 1, 169–75.
Crowe, Catherine, 1848, *The Night-Side of Nature: Or, ghosts and ghost-seers*, T.C. Newby.
Cudworth, William, 1886, *Rambles Round Horton: Historical, topographical and descriptive*, Thomas Brear.
Cunniff, Tom, 1985, *The Supernatural in Yorkshire*, Dalesman.
Czaplicka, Marie Antoinette, 1914, *Aboriginal Siberia: A study in Social Anthropology*. Oxford UP.

Dacombe, Marianne, 1935, *Dorset Up Along and Down Along*, Dorset Federation of Women's Institutes.
Dahlitz, M., and J. D. Parkes, 1993, 'Sleep paralysis', *Lancet*, 341, 406–7.
Dale-Green, Patricia, 1966, *Dog*, Rupert Hart-Davis.
Daniel, Clarence, 1973, *Ghosts of Derbyshire*, Dalesman.
Darmesteter, James, 1887, *The Zend-Avesta. Part I: The Vendîdâd*. Clarendon.
Davidson, Hilda Ellis, 1993, *The Lost Beliefs of Northern Europe*, Routledge.
Davidson, Hilda Ellis, and Anna Chaudhri (eds), 2001, *Supernatural Enemies*, Carolina Academic Press.
Dawson, W. Harbutt, 1882, *History of Skipton*, Edmondson.
Day, James Wentworth, 1954, *Here Are Ghosts and Witches*, Batsford.
Day, James Wentworth, 1958, *A Ghost-Hunter's Game-Book*, Frederick Muller.

Day, James Wentworth, 1962, 'Black Shuck', *East Anglian Magazine* 21, 638–43.

Day, James Wentworth, 1967, *Portrait of the Broads,* Robert Hale.

Day, James Wentworth, 1969, *In Search of Ghosts,* Frederick Muller.

Day, James Wentworth, 1973, *Essex Ghosts: The haunted towns and villages of Essex,* Spurbooks.

Deane, Tony, and Tony Shaw, 1975, *The Folklore of Cornwall,* Batsford.

Devereux, Paul, 2001, *Haunted Land: Investigations into ancient mysteries and modern day phenomena,* Piatkus.

Dickens, Charles, 1861, *The Uncommercial Traveller,* Chapman and Hall.

Dixon, J.H., 1881, *Chronicles and Stories of the Craven Dales,* Simpkin Marshall.

Doe, G., 1880, 'Fifth report of the committee on Devonshire folk-lore', *Tr. Of the Devonshire Assoc.,* 12, 99–113.

Drake, Francis, 1736, *Eboracum: Or the history and antiquities of the city of York,* William Bowyer.

Drew, Jacob Halls (as His Eldest Son), 1861, *Samuel Drew, MA, the Self-taught Cornishman: A life lesson,* Ward and Co.

Durston, C.A. (as Skylark Durston), 1987, *Tales from the Ragged Louse,* Artsmiths.

Dutt, William A., 1901, *Highways and Byways of East Anglia,* Macmillan.

Dutt, William A., 1903, *The Norfolk Broads,* Methuen.

Easther, Alfred, 1883, *A Glossary of the Dialect of Almondbury and Huddersfield,* (ed. Thomas Lees), English Dialect Society.

Eliade, Mircea, 1964, *Shamanism: Archaic techniques of ecstasy,* Princeton UP.

Ellis, Hilda Roderick, 1943, *The Road to Hel: A study of the conception of the dead in Old Norse literature.* Cambridge UP.

Emerson, P.H., 1888, *Pictures of East Anglian Life,* Sampson Low.

Emery, W.B., 1961, *Archaic Egypt,* Penguin.

Farson, Daniel, 1978, *The Hamlyn Book of Ghosts in Fact and Fiction,* Hamlyn.

Fauconnet, Max, 1968, 'Mythology of Black Africa' in *New Larousse Encyclopedia of Mythology* (2nd edn), Paul Hamlyn.

Field, Naomi, and Andrew White (eds), 1984, *A Prospect of Lincolnshire*, Field and White.
Fields, Kenneth, 1998, *Lancashire Magic and Mystery*, Sigma.
Findler, Gerald, 1979, *Lakeland Ghosts*, Dalesman.
Firestone, M., 1985, 'The "Old Hag": Sleep paralysis in Newfoundland', *The Journal of Psychoanalytic Anthropology*, 8, 47–66.
Fletcher, Joseph Smith, 1912, *Memories of a Spectator*, Eveleigh Nash.
Forby, Robert, 1830, *The Vocabulary of East Anglia*, J.B. Nichols and Son.
Francis, Di, 1983, *Cat Country: The quest for the British big cat*, David and Charles.

Gant, Roland, 1980, *Dorset Villages*, Robert Hale.
Gardner, Eileen, 1989, *Visions of Heaven and Hell Before Dante*, Italica.
Garner, Alan, 1969, *A Book of Goblins*, Hamish Hamilton.
Gauld, A., 1977, 'Discarnate survival', in B. B. Wolman (ed.) *Handbook of Parapsychology*, Von Nostrand Reinhold.
Gauld, A., 1982, *Mediumship and survival: A century of investigations*, Heinemann.
Gauld, A., and A.D. Cornell, 1979, *Poltergeists*, Routledge and Kegan Paul.
Gearhart, L., and M.A. Persinger, 1986, 'Geophysical variables and behavior: XXXIII. Onsets of historical and contemporary poltergeist episodes occurred with sudden increases in geomagnetic activity', *Perceptual and Motor Skills*, 62, 463–6.
Geering, Thomas (as 'One Who Has Never Lived Out Of It'), 1884, *Our Parish: A Medley*, Sussex Advertiser.
Glyde, John, (no date [1872]) *The Norfolk Garland*, London.
Goss, Mike, 1992a, 'Alien Big Cat sightings in Britain: a possible rumour legend?', *Folklore*, 103, 184–202.
Goss, Mike, 1992b, 'Black Shuck', *Fortean Times*, 63, 57.
Green, Andrew, 1973, *Our Haunted Kingdom*, Wolfe.
Green, C. E., and C. McCreery, 1975 (1989), *Apparitions*, Hamish Hamilton.
Green, Miranda, 1992, *Animals in Celtic Life and Myth*, Routledge.
Greyson, B., 2000, 'Near-death experiences' in E. Cardeña, S. J. Lynn, and S. Krippner (eds.), *Varieties of Anomalous Experience: Examining the scientific evidence*, APA.

Gunn, John, 1849, 'Proverbs, adages and popular superstitions, still preserved in the parish of Irstead', *Norfolk Archaeology* 2, 291–308.
Gurdon, Eveline Camilla, 1895, *Examples of Printed Folk-Lore Concerning Suffolk*, Folklore Society.
Gurney, E., F. W. H. Myers and F. Podmore, 1886, *Phantasms of the Living*, Trubner and Co.
Gutch, Eliza, 1901, *Examples of Printed Folk-Lore Concerning the North Riding of Yorkshire, York and the Ainsty*, Folklore Society.
Gutch, Eliza, and Mabel Peacock, 1908, *Examples of Printed Folk-Lore Concerning Lincolnshire*, Folklore Society.

Haggard, Henry Rider, 1899, *A Farmer's Year: Being his commonplace book for 1898*, Longmans Green and Co.
Haigh, Jean, 1976, 'The black dog', *Country Life*, 159, 355.
Haining, Peter, 1992, *The Supernatural Coast: Unexplained mysteries of East Anglia*, Robert Hale.
Halliday, W.R., 1954, 'The story of Sir Robert Chichester together with a note on the Rev. William Gimmingham', *Folk-Lore*, 65, 109–111.
Hannah, I.C., 1932, 'Philpots camp, West Hoathly', *Sussex Arch. Coll.* 73, 156–67.
Haraldsson, E., 1985, 'Representative national surveys of psychic phenomena: Iceland, Great Britain, Sweden, USA and Gallup's multinational survey', *Journal of the Society for Psychical Research*, 53, 145–58.
Haraldsson, E., 1994, 'Apparitions of the dead: analysis of a new collection of 350 reports', in E. W. Cook and D. L. Delanoy (eds.), *Research in Parapsychology 1991*, Scarecrow Press.
Hardwick, Charles, 1872, *Traditions, Superstitions and Folk-Lore: Chiefly Lancashire and the North of England*, Simpkin Marshall.
Hare, Augustus, 1896–1900, *The Story of My Life*, George Allen; abridged edition published 1953 as *In My Solitary Life*, (ed. M. barnes, Allen and Unwin.
Harland, John, and Thomas Turner Wilkinson, 1867, *Lancashire Folk-Lore*, Frederick Warne.
Harries, John, 1968, *The Ghost Hunter's Road Book*, Frederick Muller.
Hart, H., 1956, 'Six theories about apparitions', *Proceedings of the Society for Psychical Research*, 50, 153–239.

Harte, Jeremy, 1986, *Cuckoo Pounds and Singing Barrows: The folklore of archaeological sites in Dorset*, Dorset Natural History and Archaeological Society.

Harte, Jeremy, 1995, 'On the trail of the Black Dog', *Wisht Maen* 4, 2–6.

Harte, T. M., D.L. Black, M.T. Hollishead, and D. Mitchell, 2001, 'MESA: multi-energy sensor array in a baseline vs. haunt site', *Proceedings of the 44th Parapsychological Association Convention*, 135–46.

Hayward, L.H., 1938, 'Shropshire folklore of yesterday and to-day', *Folk-Lore* 49, 223–43

Henderson, William, 1879, *Notes on the Folk-Lore of the Northern Counties of England and the Borders*, Folklore Society.

Hewett, Sarah, 1900, *Nummits and Crummits: Devonshire customs, characteristics and folk-lore*, Thomas Burleigh.

Hole, Christina, 1937, *Traditions and Customs of Cheshire*, Williams and Norgate.

Hole, Christina, 1940a, *English Folklore*, Batsford.

Hole, Christina, 1940b, *Haunted England: A survey of English ghost-lore*, Batsford.

Hone, William, 1827–8, *The Table Book*, William Hone.

Hood, Christobel M., *et al*, 1926, 'Scraps of English folklore: XV', *Folk-Lore* 37, 364–71.

Hooper, James, 1894, 'Demon Dogs of Norfolk and Suffolk,' *Eastern Daily Press*, 2, 5 July.

Hope, Robert Charles, 1893, *The Legendary Lore of Holy Wells*, Elliot Stock.

Hopkins, B., D.M. Jacobs and R. Westrum, 1992, *Unusual Personal Experiences: An analysis of the data from three national surveys conducted by the Roper Organization*, Bigelow Holding Corporation.

Houran, J., and R. Lange, 1996, 'Hauntings and poltergeist-like episodes as a confluence of conventional phenomena', *Perceptual and Motor Skills*, 83, 1307–16.

Houran, J., and R. Lange, 1998, 'Rationale and application of a multi-energy sensory array in the investigation of haunting and poltergeist cases', *Journal of the Society for Psychical Research*, 62, 324–36.

Houran, J., and R. Lange (eds.), 2001, *Hauntings and Poltergeists: Multidisciplinary perspectives*, McFarland.

Huddleston, N.A., 2004, 'Black Dogs', *FLS News* 43, 16.

Huff, Chris, 2002, '*Cave canem*', *Anomaly (the ASSAP Journal)* 30, 2–19.

Hufford, D. J., 1982, *The Terror that Comes in the Night: An experience-centered study of supernatural assault traditions,* University of Pennsylvania Press.

Hultkrantz, Åke, 1957, *The North American Indian Orpheus Tradition: A contribution to comparative religion.* Stockholm.

Humphreys, Arthur L., 1889, *Materials for the History of the Town of Wellington, Co. Somerset,* Henry Gray.

Hurren, A., 1994, 'The tale of Black Shuck,' *Eastern Daily Press,* 11, 26 September.

Innes, Simon, 1983a, 'Beware of the dog', *The Unexplained,* 86,1710–13

Innes, Simon, 1983b 'Tracking down the Black Dog', *The Unexplained* 87,1730–3.

Irwin, H. J., 1994, 'The phenomenology of parapsychological experiences' in S. Krippner (ed.), *Advances in Parapsychological Research Vol. 7,* McFarland.

Irwin, H. J., 1999, *An Introduction to Parapsychology* (3rd ed.), McFarland.

Jackson, Thomas, 1855, *The Life of the Rev. Robert Newton, DD,* John Mason

James, M.H., 1891, *Bogie Tales of East Anglia,* Pawsey and Hayes.

Jefferies, Richard, 1879, *Wild Life in a Southern County,* Smith, Elder and Co.

Jeffrey, Martin, 2004, 'Black dog legends'; downloaded July 2004 from www.mysterymag.com/earthmysteries/index.php.

Jenkins, Stephen, 1977, *The Undiscovered Country: Adventures into other dimensions,* Neville Spearman.

Jennings, Pete, 1994, 'Black Shuck legends', *Gippeswic,* 9, 2–5.

Jewitt, W. Henry, 1903, 'Oxfordshire folk-lore', *Folk-Lore* 14, 183–5.

Jochelsen, Waldemar, 1904, *The Koryak.* New York.

Jochelsen, Waldemar, 1924, *The Yukaghir and the Yukaghirized Tungus.* New York.

Johnson, Walter, 1936–7, 'Marshland notions sixty years ago: I', *Lincolnshire Magazine,* 3, 83–6.

Jones, Edmund, 2003, *The Appearance of Evil: Apparitions of spirits in Wales,* (ed. John Harvey), University of Wales Press.

Jordan, Katy, 2000, *The Haunted Landscape: Folklore, ghosts and legends of Wiltshire,* Ex Libris.

Kent, Charles, 1910, *The Land of the 'Babes In The Wood': Or, the Breckland of Norfolk*, Jarrold.
Kittredge, George Lyman, 1929, *Witchcraft in Old and New England*, Harvard UP.
Knight, Stephen, 1994, *Robin Hood: A complete study of the English outlaw*, Blackwell.
Knights, M., 1889, *The Norfolk and Norwich Annual 1889*, Norwich.

Larwood, Jacob, and John Camden Hotten, 1866, *The History of Signboards: From the earliest times to the present day*, John Camden Hotten.
Leach, Maria, 1961, *God Had a Dog: Folklore of the dog*, Rutgers UP.
Leaning, F. E., 1925, 'An introductory study of hypnagogic phenomena', *Proceedings of the Society for Psychical Research*, 35, 287–411.
Leather, Ella Mary, 1912, *The Folk-Lore of Herefordshire*, Jakeman and Carver.
Leese, Philip R., 1989, *The Kidsgrove Boggart and the Black Dog*, Staffordshire Libraries.
Lewis, R.E., *et al.* (eds), 1987, *The Middle English Dictionary*, Part S.6, University of Michigan Press.
Liddon, S. C., 1967, 'Sleep paralysis and hypnagogic hallucinations: their relationship to the nightmare', *Archives of General Psychiatry*, 17, 88–96.
Linahan, Liz, 1994, *Pit Ghosts, Padfeet and Poltergeists: Stories, tales and legends of the South Yorkshire Area*, Kings England.
Lincoln, Bruce, 1991a, 'Mithra(s) as sun and saviour' in B. Lincoln, *Death, War, and Sacrifice: Studies in ideology and practice*, University of Chicago Press; originally published in Ugo Bianchi and M.J. Vermaseren (eds), *La Soteriologia dei Culti Orientali nell' Impero Romano*, Leiden (1982).
Lincoln, Bruce, 1991b, 'The Hellhound', in B. Lincoln, *Death, War, and Sacrifice: Studies in ideology and practice*, University of Chicago Press; originally published in the *Journal of Indo-European Studies*, 7 (1979).
Lofthouse, Jessica, 1976, *North Country Folklore: In Lancashire, Cumbria and the Pennine Dales*, Robert Hale.
Longstaffe, William H.D., 1854, *The History and Antiquities of the Parish of Darlington, in the Bishopric*, Henry Parker.
Loveday, R., ?1960s, Collection of newspaper cuttings 1950s–70s, some undated. Jennifer Westwood collection.

Lower, Mark Anthony, 1861, 'Old speech and old manners in Sussex', *Sussex Archaeological Collections,* 13, 209–36.
Lucas, Joseph, 1882, *Studies in Nidderdale,* T. Thorpe.

'M., Alice', 1870, 'Western England folk lore', *Notes and Queries,* 4 ser. 6, 497–8.
McClenon, J., 1991, 'Social science and anomalous experience: paradigms for investigating sporadic social phenomena', *Journal of the American Society for Psychical Research*, 85, 25–41.
McClenon, J., 1994a, 'Surveys of anomalous experience: a cross-cultural analysis, *Journal of the American Society for Psychical Research*, 88, 117–35.
McClenon, J., 1994b, *Wondrous Events: Foundations of religious belief*, University of Pennsylvania Press.
McCue, Peter A., 2002, 'Theories of haunting: a critical overview', *Journal of the Society for Psychical Research*, 66, 1–21.
McEwan, Graham J., 1986, *Mystery Animals of Britain and Ireland,* Robert Hale.
MacGregor, Alasdair Alpin, 1955, *The Ghost Book: Strange happenings in Britain*, Robert Hale.
McGrory, David, 1995, 'On the sniff', *Fortean Times,* 83, 42–3.
MacKenzie, A., 1982, *Hauntings and Apparitions,* Heinemann.
Mackie, Charles, 1904–5, 'A budget of Christmas tales', *Norfolk and Norwich Notes and Queries,* 3 ser. 1, 103–7.
MacQuoid, Thomas and Katharine, 1883, *About Yorkshire,* Chatto and Windus.
Maher, M. C., 2000, 'Quantitative investigation of the General Wayne Inn', *Journal of Parapsychology*, 64, 365–90.
Maher, M. C. and G.P. Hansen, 1997, 'Quantitative investigation of a legally disputed "haunted house"', *The Parapsychological Association 40th Annual Convention Proceedings of Presented Papers,* 184–201.
Maloret, Nick, 1987, 'Another golden oldie', *Fortean Times,* 48, 17.
Maple, Eric, 1964, *The Realm of Ghosts,* Robert Hale.
Marlowe, Christopher, 1927, *People and Places in Marshland,* Cecil Palmer.
Marryat, Frederick, 1837, *Snarly-yow or the Dog-fiend,* Meline, Cans and Cie.
Mathews, F.W., 1923, *Tales of the Blackdown Borderland,* Somerset Folk Press.

Mavromatis, A., 1987, *Hypnagogia: The unique state of consciousness between wakefulness and sleep*, Routledge and Kegan Paul.
'M.E.R.' 1955–6, 'An outing in Dorset', *Dorset Year Book* 1955–6, 119–25.
Michell, John, and Bob Rickard, 1977, *Phenomena*, Thames and Hudson.
Miles, Clarissa, 1907–8, 'Experiments in thought transference', *Journal of the Society for Psychical Research*, 13, 243–62.
Miller, Keith, 1984, 'The Black Dog and other canine apparitions in Lincolnshire', in N. Field and A. White (eds), *A Prospect of Lincolnshire*, Field and White.
Mitchell, W.R., 1969, *Haunted Yorkshire*, Dalesman Books.
Mitchell, W.R., 1973, *Yorkshire Ghosts*, Dalesman Books.
Moody, Raymond A., 1994, 'A latter-day psychomanteum', *The Parapsychological Association 37th Annual Convention Proceedings of Presented Papers*, 335–6.
Moody, Raymond with Paul Perry, 1993, *Reunions: Visionary encounters with departed loved ones*, Little, Brown and Company.
Moor, Edward, 1823, *Suffolk Words and Phrases: Or, an attempt to collect the lingual localisms of that county*, J. Loder.
Moore, Steve, 1976, 'Notes on Greenwich phenomena: III', *Fortean Times*, 16, 8–12.
Moorman, Frederic William, ed, 1916, *Yorkshire Dialect Poems 1673–1915: And traditional poems*, Yorkshire Dialect Society.
Morris, M.C.F., 1892, *Yorkshire Folk-Talk: With characteristics of those who speak it in the North and East Ridings*, Henry Frowde.

Needle, Rex, 2001, 'Bourne diary'; downloaded July 2004 from http://homepages.which.net/~rex/bourne/diary200108.htm.
Neppe, V. M., 1990, 'Anomalistic experience and the cerebral cortex', in S. Krippner (ed.), *Advances in Parapsychological Research Vol. 6*, McFarland.
Ness, R. C., 1978, 'The Old Hag phenomenon as sleep paralysis: a biocultural interpretation', *Culture, Medicine and Psychiatry*, 2, 15–39.
Newman, L.F., and E.M. Wilson, 1952, 'Folklore survivals in the southern 'Lake Counties' and in Essex: a comparison and contrast', *Folk-Lore*, 63, 91–104.

Newton, Sam, 1993, *The Origins of* Beowulf *and the Pre-Viking Kingdom of East Anglia,* D.S. Brewer.
Nichols, John, 1795–1815, *The History and Antiquities of the County of Leicester,* J.B. Nichols.
Nichols, John, 1828, *Illustrations of the Literary History of the Eighteenth Century,* J.B. Nichols.
Nicholson, John, 1890, *Folk Lore of East Yorkshire,* Simpkin Marshall.
North, Mark, 2003, 'Tracking down Dorset's Black Dogs', *Centre for Fortean Zoology Yearbook* 2003, 1–18.

O'Donnell, Elliot, 1948, *Haunted Britain,* Rider.
O'Donnell, Petronella, 1923, 'Eerie spots in Somerset', *Somerset Year Book,* 22, 20–4
O'Donnell, Petronella, 1934, 'Superstition in the West', *Somerset Year Book,* 33, 102–6.
Oates, Caroline, and Juliette Wood, 1998, *A Coven of Scholars: Margaret Murray and her working methods,* Folklore Society.
Ojoade, J. Olowo, 1990, 'Nigerian cultural attitudes to the dog', in Roy Willis (ed.), *Signifying Animals: Human meaning in the natural world,* Routledge.
Olivier, Edith, and Margaret K.S. Edwards (eds), 1930, *Moonrakings: A little book of Wiltshire stories,* Coates and Parker.
Osis, K., 1986, 'Characteristics of purposeful action in an apparition case', *Journal of the American Society for Psychical Research,* 80, 175–93.
Osis, K., and E. Haraldsson, 1986, 'Deathbed observations by physicians and nurses: a cross-cultural survey', *Journal of the American Society for Psychical Research,* 71, 237–59.
Owen, D.D.R., 1970, *The Vision of Hell: Infernal journeys in medieval French literature.* Scottish Academic Press.
Owen, Gale R., 1981, *Rites and Religions of the Anglo-Saxons,* David and Charles.

Palmer, J., 1979, 'A community mail survey of psychic experiences', *Journal of the American Society for Psychical Research,* 73, 221–51.
Palmer, Kingsley, 1973, *Oral Folk-Tales of Wessex,* David and Charles.
Palmer, Roy, 1976, *The Folklore of Warwickshire,* Batsford.
Palmer, Roy, 1985, *Folklore of Leicestershire and Rutland,* Sycamore Press.

Palmer, Roy, 1994, *The Folklore of Gloucestershire,* Westcountry Books.
Parish, R.B., 1998, 'Black Dogs, phantom felines and other strange manifestations', *Bygone Kent,* 19, 79–83.
Parke, Aubrey L., 1963 'The folklore of Sixpenny Handley, Dorset', *Folklore,* 74, 481–7.
Parkinson, Thomas, 1888–9, *Yorkshire Legends and Traditions: As told by her ancient chronicles, her poets, and journalists,* Elliot Stock.
Parrinder, Geoffrey, 1982, *African Mythology* (2nd ed.), Hamlyn.
Partridge, J.B., 1912, 'Cotswold place-lore and customs: I', *Folk-Lore,* 23, 332–42.
Peacock, Edward, 1877, *A Glossary of Words Used in the Wapentakes of Manley and Corringham, Lincolnshire,* English Dialect Society.
Peacock, Edward, 1898, 'The Devil as a black dog', *Notes and Queries,* 9 ser. 2, 335–6.
Peacock, Mabel (as P.M.), 1894–5, 'Animal apparitions in Lincolnshire', *Lincolnshire Notes and Queries,* 4, 146–9.
Pegge, Samuel, 1896, *Two Collections of Derbicisms,* (ed. Walter Skeat and Thomas Hallam), English Dialect Society.
Pendleton, David, 1986, 'Spectral brew', *Earth,* 3, 16.
Persinger, M. A., 1974, *The Paranormal. Part I: Patterns,* MSS Information Corporation.
Persinger, M. A., 1989, 'Psi phenomena and temporal lobe activity: the geomagnetic factor', in L. A. Henkel and R. Berger (eds.), *Research in Parapsychology 1988,* Scarecrow Press.
Persinger, M. A., and S.A. Koren, 2001, 'Predicting the characteristics of haunt phenomena from geomagnetic factors and brain sensitivity: evidence from field and experimental studies', in J. Houran, and R. Lange (eds.), *Hauntings and Poltergeists: Multidisciplinary perspectives,* McFarland.
Pettersson, Olof, 1957, *Jabmek and Jabmeaimo: A comparative study of the dead and the realm of the dead in Lappish religion,* Lund.
Porter, Enid, 1969, *Cambridgeshire Customs and Folklore,* Routledge and Kegan Paul.
Porter, Enid, 1974, *The Folklore of East Anglia,* Batsford.
Porter, J.R., and W.M.S. Russell (eds), 1978, *Animals in Folklore,* Folklore Society.
Powell, John U., 1901, 'Folklore notes from South-West Wilts', *Folk-Lore,* 12, 71–83.

Price, H. H., 1938–9, 'Haunting and the "Psychic Ether" hypothesis', *Proceedings of the Society for Psychical Research*, 45, 307–41.

Priest, Vicki, Patrick Clay and J.D. Hill, 2003, 'Iron Age gold in Leicestershire', *Current Archaeology,* 188, 358–62.

Priest, Vicki and Patrick Clay, 2004, 'The East Leicestershire hoard', *Transactions of the Leicestershire Archaeological and Historical Society*, 78, 141–2.

Puhvel, Martin, 1989, *The Crossroads in Folklore and Myth.* P. Lang.

'Q.', 1910–11, 'Northumbrian ghost stories', *The Treasury,* 16, 389–95.

Radin, D. I., 2001, 'Seeking spirits in the laboratory', in J. Houran and R. Lange (eds.), *Hauntings and Poltergeists: Multidisciplinary perspectives*, McFarland.

Radin, D. I., and J.M. Rebman, 1996, 'Are phantasms fact or fantasy? A preliminary investigation of apparitions evoked in the laboratory', *Journal of the Society for Psychical Research*, 61, 65–87.

Radin, D. I., and W.G. Roll, 1996, 'Investigation of two haunted castles in Scandinavia', *The Parapsychological Association 39th Annual Convention Proceedings of Presented Papers*, 271–8.

Rae-Ellis, Vivienne, 1990, *True Ghost Stories of Our Time*, Faber and Faber.

Rajaram, M., and S. Mitra, 1981, 'Correlations between convulsive seizures and geomagnetic activity', *Neuroscience Letters*, 24, 187–91.

Randell, Arthur R., 1966, *Sixty Years a Fenman*, (ed. Enid Porter), Routledge and Kegan Paul.

Raven, Jon, 1978, *The Folklore of Staffordshire*, Batsford.

Readers' Digest, 1977, *Folklore, Myths and Legends of Britain*, (2nd edn).

Rees, W. D., 1971, 'The hallucinations of widowhood', *British Medical Journal*, 4, 37–41.

Reeve, Christopher, 1988, A Straunge and Terrible Wunder*: The story of the Black Dog of Bungay*, Morrow and Co.

Rice-Heaps, Victoria, 2002, 'Black Shuck seen', *Fortean Times,* 154, 52–3.

Rider Haggard, H., 1899, *A Farmer's Year.* London.

Rickard, Bob, 1981, 'Out of place', *Fortean Times,* 35, 44–5.

Rickard, Bob, 1983, 'The Exmoor Beast and others', *Fortean Times,* 40, 52 61.

Ritson, Joseph, 1831, *Fairy Tales,* Payne & Foss.

Robinson, C.C. (anonymously), 1862, *The Dialect of Leeds and its Neighbourhood,* John Russell Smith.

Robinson, F.K, 1876, *A Glossary of Words Used in the Neighbourhood of Whitby,* English Dialect Society.

Rogers, Charles (as Wold Charl), 1926, 'To Darset Men athirt th'zeas', *Dorset Year Book 1926,* 126–139.

Rogers, Ken, 1994, *The Warminster Triangle: Astounding UFO and crop circle sightings,* Coates and Parker.

Roll, W. G., and M.A. Persinger, 2001, 'Investigations of poltergeists and haunts: a review and interpretation', in J. Houran, and R. Lange (eds.), *Hauntings and Poltergeists: Multidisciplinary perspectives,* McFarland.

Rudkin, Ethel H., 1938, 'The Black Dog', *Folk-Lore* 49, 111–31.

Rudkin, Ethel H., 1955, 'Folklore of Lincolnshire: especially the low-lying areas of Lindsey', *Folk-Lore,* 66, 385–400.

Rye, Walter, 1872–3, 'Norfolk superstitions', *Eastern Counties Collectanea,* 2, 2–4.

Rye, Walter, 1877, 'The prophecies, traditions, superstitions, folklore, sayings, and rhymes of Norfolk', *The Norfolk Antiquarian Miscellany,* 1, 285–311.

Rye, Walter, 1895, *A Glossary of Words used in East Anglia founded on that of Forby,* English Dialect Society Original Glossaries No.75.

Rye, Walter, 1897, *Songs, Stories, and Sayings of Norfolk.* Norwich.

Rye, Walter, 1920, *The Recreations of a Norfolk Antiquary,* H.W. Hunt.

'R.J.K.', 1850, 'Local rhymes and proverbs of Devonshire', *Notes and Queries,* 1 ser. 2, 511–3.

Salim, Valerie, 1983, *Ghost Hunters' Guide to Sheffield,* Sheaf.

Sanders, John, 1984, 'Some New Forest mysteries', *Earth Giant,* 4, 3–4

Saxo Grammaticus, (1979), *History of the Danes. I: Text* (trans. Peter Fisher and ed. Hilda Ellis Davidson), Brewer.

Schacter, D. L., 1976, 'The hypnagogic state: a critical review of the literature', *Psychological Bulletin,* 83, 452–81.

Sheils, D., 1978, 'A cross-cultural study of beliefs in out-of-the-body experiences, waking and sleeping', *Journal of the Society for Psychical Research,* 49, 697–741.

Shepherd, Val, 1994, *Historic Wells In and Around Bradford*, Heart of Albion.

Sherwood, S. J., 2000a, *Modelling Childhood Antecedents of Anomalous Experiences and Beliefs: Fantasy proneness, hypnagogic/ hypnopompic and sleep experiences.* Unpublished PhD thesis, University of Edinburgh.

Sherwood, S. J., 2000b, 'A comparison of the features of the psychomanteum and hypnagogic/ hypnopompic experiences', *International Journal of Parapsychology,* 11, 97-121.

Sherwood, S. J., 2000c, 'Black Dogs and English men', *Exceptional Human Experience,* 16, 226–30.

Sherwood, S. J., 2000d, 'Black Dog Apparitions', *Journal of the American Society for Psychical Research,* 94, 151–64.

Sherwood, S. J.,2002a, 'Apparitions of black dogs', *Paranormal Review,* 22, 3–6.

Sherwood, S.J., 2002b, 'Relationship between the hypnagogic/ hypnopompic states and reports of anomalous experiences', *Journal of Parapsychology,* 66, 127–50.

Sidgwick, H., A. Johnson, F.W.H. Myers, F. Podmore and E.M. Sidgwick, 1894, 'Report on the Census of Hallucinations', *Proceedings of the Society for Psychical Research,* 10, 25–422.

Siikala, Anna-Leena, 2002, *Mythic Images and Shamanism: A perspective on Kalevala poetry,* Helsinki.

Simek, Rudolf, 1993, *Dictionary of Northern Mythology,* Brewer.

Simon-Buller, S., V.A. Christopherson and R.A.Jones,1988, 'Correlates of sensing the presence of a deceased spouse', *Omega,* 190, 21–30.

Simpson, Jacqueline, 1973, *The Folklore of Sussex,* Batsford.

Simpson, Jacqueline, 2003, 'Repentant soul or walking corpse? Debatable apparitions in medieval England', *Folklore,* 114, 389–402.

Simpson, Jacqueline, and Steve Roud, 2000, *A Dictionary of English Folklore,* Oxford UP.

Smith, Grace Partridge, 1938, 'An anecdote from Hampshire', *Folk-Lore,* 49, 161–5

Smith, Worthing G., 1904, *Dunstable: Its history and surroundings,* Elliot Stock.

Snell, F.J., 1903, *A Book of Exmoor,* Methuen.

Southwart, Elizabeth, 1923, *Brontë Moors and Villages from Thornton to Haworth,* John Lane.

Speight, Harry, 1902, *Lower Wharfedale*, Elliot Stock.
Spencer, A.J., 1982, *Death in Ancient Egypt*, Penguin.
Spencer, John and Anne, 2001, *The Encyclopedia of Ghosts and Spirits II*, Headline.
Spooner, Barbara C., 1925–30a, 'The dog called 'Darley' ', *Old Cornwall*, 1viii, 23–6.
Spooner, Barbara C., 1925–30b, 'The dog in the lane', *Old Cornwall*, 1xii, 25–8.
St Leger-Gordon, Ruth, 1965, *The Witchcraft and Folklore of Dartmoor*, Robert Hale.
Staveley, David, 2002, 'Ghostly Black Dogs'; downloaded July 2004 from www.prestel.co.uk/aspen/sussex/blackdog.html.
Stevenson, I., 1982, 'The contribution of apparitions to the evidence for survival', *Journal of the American Society for Psychical Research*, 76, 341–58.
Stone, Alby, 1998, 'The road that makes things disappear: the path of the dead in Indo-European myth and religion.' *Fortean Studies*, 5, 122–35.
Stone, Alby, 2003, *Explore Shamanism*, Heart of Albion.
Suffling, Ernest R., 1891, *History and Legends of the Broad District*, Jarrold.
Sullivan, J., 1857, *Cumberland and Westmoreland, Ancient and Modern: The people, dialect, superstitions and customs*, Whittaker.
Swift, Eric, 1954, *Folktales of the East Midlands*, Thomas Nelson.

Tandy, V., 2000, 'Something in the cellar', *Journal of the Society for Psychical Research*, 64, 129–40.
Tandy, V., and T.R. Lawrence, 1998, 'The ghost in the machine', *Journal of the Society for Psychical Research*, 62, 360–4.
Taylor, David, 1995, 'The hounds of Woden', *Mercian Mysteries*, 22, 18.
Taylor, E.S., 1850, 'Shuck the dog-fiend', *Notes and Queries* 1 ser. 1, 468.
Taylor, Francis, 1901, *The Folk-Speech of South Lancashire*, John Heywood.
Taylor, Ian, 1990, 'Otherworlds around us', *Earth*, 15, 8–9.
Taylor, Ian, 1991, 'The Gytrash of Goathland and other fragments', *Northern Earth Mysteries*, 48, 15–20.
'T.D.P.', 1864, 'Norfolk folk lore', *Notes and Queries* 3 ser. 5, 236–7.
Tebbult, L.F, 1945, 'A Buckinghamshire Black Dog', *Folk-Lore*, 56, 222.

Thelwall, M., 1900–1, 'The power of darkness', *The Eastern Counties Magazine,* 1, 291–8.
Thomas, Keith, 1973, *Religion and the Decline of Magic,* Charles Schribner's Sons.
Thomas, Keith, 1984, *Man and the Natural World: Changing attitudes in England 1500–1800,* Penguin.
Thompson, G.E., 2000, 'Black Shuck?', *Fortean Times,* 138, 50.
Thompson, Stith, 1955–8, *Motif-Index of Folk-Literature,* Indiana UP.
Thornton, W.H., 1897, *Reminiscences of an Old West Country Clergyman,* Andrew Iredale.
Todd, Simon, 2000, 'The Billingham incident'; downloaded July 2004 from http://members.sniffout.com/simontodd/billigm.htm.
Tongue, Ruth, 1956, 'Traces of fairy hounds in Somerset', *Folk-Lore,* 67, 233–4.
Tongue, Ruth, 1965, *Somerset Folklore* (ed. Katharine M. Briggs), Folklore Society.
Tongue, Ruth, 1970, *Forgotten Folk-Tales of the English Counties* (ed. Katharine M. Briggs), Routledge and Kegan Paul.
Trubshaw, Bob, 1994a, 'Black Dogs in folklore', *Mercian Mysteries,* 20, 8–10; online at www.indigogroup.co.uk/edge/bdogfl.htm
Trubshaw, Bob, 1994b, 'Black Dogs: guardians of the corpse ways', *Mercian Mysteries,* 20, 16–27; online at www.indigogroup.co.uk/edge/bdogs.htm
Tudor, Sean, 2004, 'Road ghosts'; downloaded July 2004 from www.roadghosts.com
Turner, Mark, 1993, *Folklore and Mysteries of the Cotswolds,* Robert Hale.
Turville-Petre, E.O.G., 1964, *Myth and Religion of the North: The religion of ancient Scandinavia.* Weidenfeld and Nicolson.
Tyrrell, G. N. M., 1943 (1973), *Apparitions,* The Society for Psychical Research.

Van Leiburg, Fred, 2003, 'Ghosts, animals or angels: Christian story-telling in a modern world', *Folklore (the Journal of the Estonian Literary Museum),* 20, 17–37.

Walcott, Mackenzie E.C., 1861, *The East Coast of England,* Edward Stanford.
Wales, Tony, 1992, *Sussex Ghosts and Legends,* Countryside Books.
Waring, Edward, 1966, 'The Black Dog in Dorset', *Proc. of the Dorset Nat. Hist. and Arch. Soc.,* 88, 234.

Waring, Edward, 1977, *Ghosts and Legends of the Dorset Countryside*, Compton Press.
Watson, C. Somerville, 1922, 'The Kirk Grim: a legend of Burlington, Somersetshire', *Somerset Year Book,* 21, 48–9.
Watson, Sam, 1997, 'Black Dog, Big Cat – or Barguest?', *Northern Earth,* 69, 7–11.
Way, A. (ed.), 1865, *Promptorium Parvulorum,* Camden Society.
Welby, Alfred, 1934–5, 'The White Dog of Eresby', *Lincolnshire Notes and Queries,* 23, 132–3.
Wender, Dorothea (trans.), 1973, *Hesiod and Theognis,* Penguin.
Westwood, Jennifer, 1985, *Albion: A Guide to Legendary Britain,* Granada.
Westwood, Jennifer, 2001, 'Friend or foe? Norfolk traditions of Shuck', in H.E. Davidson and A. Chaudhri (eds), *Supernatural Enemies,* Carolina Academic Press; reprinted in the present volume.
Whistler, C.W., 1908, 'Local traditions of the Quantocks', *Folk-Lore,* 19, 31–51.
White, David Gordon, 1991, *Myths of the Dog-Man,* University of Chicago Press.
Whiteside, Joseph, 1904, *Shappe in Bygone Days,* Titus Wilson.
'Wiccawillow', 2004, 'I used to live in a tiny village...'; downloaded July 2004 from www.healthypages.net/forum/tm.asp?m=77159
Wilkinson, H. P., and A. Gauld, 1993, 'Geomagnetism and anomalous experiences, 1868–1980', *Proceedings of the Society for Psychical Research,* 57, 275–310.
Wilkinson, Tattersall, 1904–5, 'Local folk lore', *Reports of the Halifax Antiquarian Society* 1904–5, 2–9.
Wilkinson, Tattersall, and J.F. Tattersall, 1889, *Memories of Hurstwood, Burnley, Lancashire,* J.S. Virtue.
Wilkinson, Thomas Turner, 1850, '"Trash" or "Skriker"', *Notes and Queries,* 1 ser. 2, 52–3.
Williams, B. J., 2001, 'The ghost in the mind: a brain-environment interaction model of the apparitional experience', *Proceedings of the 44th Parapsychological Association Convention,* 364–76.
Williams, David, 1994, 'Devil dogs of the British Isles', *Dead of Night,* 3, 4–10.
Williams, David, 1995, 'The Barguest and other black dog tales', *Dead of Night,* 4, 4–10.

Williamson, Cecil, 1995, 'Close encounter with a demon hound', *The Cauldron,* 78, 11–12.

Wilson, David, 1992, *Anglo-Saxon Paganism,* Routledge.

Wiltshire, Kathleen, 1973, *Ghosts and Legends of the Wiltshire Countryside,* Colin Venton.

Wiltshire, Kathleen, 1984, *More Ghosts and Legends of the Wiltshire Countryside* (ed. Patricia Carrott), Colin Venton.

Wiseman, R., C. Watt, E. Greening, P. Stevens, and C. O'Keeffe, 2003, 'An investigation into alleged "hauntings"', *British Journal of Psychology,* 94, 195–211.

Witcutt, W.P., 1942, 'Notes on Staffordshire folklore', *Folk-Lore,* 53, 126–7.

Woodley, Helen, 1994, 'Site saving', *The Ley Hunter,* 122, 33.

Woods, Barbara Allen, 1959, *The Devil in Dog Form: A partial type-index of devil legends,* University of California Press.

Woodward, James M., 1866, *The History of Bordesley Abbey, in the Valley of the Arrow,* J.H. & H. Parker.

Wright, Joseph, 1898, *The English Dialect Dictionary,* Henry Frowde.

Index

N.B. The bibliography (pages 99–128) has not been indexed.

Sacred Places:

Prehistory and popular imagination

Bob Trubshaw

Sacred Places asks why certain types of prehistoric places are thought of as sacred, and explores how the physical presence of such sacred sites is less important than what these places signify. So this is not another guide book to sacred places but instead provides a unique and thought-provoking guide to the mental worlds – the mindscapes – in which we have created the idea of prehistoric sacred places.

Recurring throughout this book is the idea that we continually create and re-create our ideas about the past, about landscapes, and the places within those landscapes that we regard as sacred. For example, although such concepts as 'nature', 'landscape', 'countryside', 'rural' and the contrast between profane and sacred are all part of our everyday thinking, in this book Bob Trubshaw shows they are all modern cultural constructions which act as the 'unseen' foundations on which we construct more complex myths about places.

Key chapters look at how earth mysteries, modern paganism and other alternative approaches to sacred places developed in recent decades, and also outline the recent dramatic changes within academic archaeology. Is there now a 'middle way' between academic and alternative approaches which recognises that what we know about the past is far less significant than what we believe about the past?

Bob Trubshaw has been actively involved with academic and alternative approaches to archaeology for most of the last twenty years. In 1996 he founded *At the Edge* magazine to popularise new interpretations of past and place.

ISBN 1 872883 67 2. Published 2005.
275 x 175 mm, 203 + xiv pages, 43 b&w illustrations and 7 line drawings, paperback. **£16.95**

Also from Heart of Albion Press

Explore Fairy Traditions

Jeremy Harte

We are not alone. In the shadows of our countryside there lives a fairy race, older than humans, and not necessarily friendly to them. For hundreds of years, men and women have told stories about the strange people, beautiful as starlight, fierce as wolves, and heartless as ice. These are not tales for children. They reveal the fairies as a passionate, proud, brutal people.

Explore Fairy Traditions draws on legends, ballads and testimony from throughout Britain and Ireland to reveal what the fairies were really like. It looks at changelings, brownies, demon lovers, the fairy host, and abduction into the Otherworld. Stories and motifs are followed down the centuries to reveal the changing nature of fairy lore, as it was told to famous figures like W.B. Yeats and Sir Walter Scott. All the research is based on primary sources and many errors about fairy tradition are laid to rest.

Jeremy Harte combines folklore scholarship with a lively style to show what the presence of fairies meant to people's lives. Like their human counterparts, the secret people could kill as well as heal. They knew marriage, seduction, rape and divorce; they adored some children and rejected others. If we are frightened of the fairies, it may be because their world offers an uncomfortable mirror of our own.

'*Explore Fairy Traditions* is an excellent introduction to the folklore of fairies, and I would highly recommend it.' Paul Mason *Silver Wheel*

ISBN 1 872883 61 3. **Published 2004.**
Demi 8vo (215 x 138 mm), 171 + vi pages, 6 line drawings, paperback. **£9.95**

Explore Shamanism

Alby Stone

Shamanism is a complex and confusing subject. There are many different ideas about what shamanism is, who is a shaman, and what a shaman does. *Explore Shamanism* provides a much-needed up-to-date guide to the study of shamanism.

Focusing mainly on the shamans of Siberia and Central Asia, *Explore Shamanism* includes a historical survey of academic approaches to shamanism, an overview of the various theories about shamanism, and a discussion of the origins of shamanism based on the latest ideas. There are also more detailed explorations of the initiation of shamans; the costumes, drums and other tools of the shaman's trade; journeys to the spirit world; and the place of trance, spirit possession and ecstasy in shamanic performance.

Explore Shamanism also surveys revived and reconstructed shamanisms in the world today.

Alby Stone has been studying and writing about shamanism for twenty years.

ISBN 1 872883 68 0. Published 2003.
Perfect bound, Demi 8vo (215 x 138 mm), 184 + x pages, 2 photographs; 17 line drawings, **£9.95**

Also from Heart of Albion Press

Explore Folklore

Bob Trubshaw

'A howling success, which plugs a big and obvious gap'

Professor Ronald Hutton

There have been fascinating developments in the study of folklore in the last twenty-or-so years, but few books about British folklore and folk customs reflect these exciting new approaches. As a result there is a huge gap between scholarly approaches to folklore studies and 'popular beliefs' about the character and history of British folklore. *Explore Folklore* is the first book to bridge that gap, and to show how much 'folklore' there is in modern day Britain.

Explore Folklore shows there is much more to folklore than morris dancing and fifty-something folksingers! The rituals of 'what we do on our holidays', funerals, stag nights and 'lingerie parties' are all full of 'unselfconscious' folk customs. Indeed, folklore is something that is integral to all our lives – it is so intrinsic we do not think of it as being 'folklore'.

The implicit ideas underlying folk lore and customs are also explored. There might appear to be little in common between people who touch wood for luck (a 'tradition' invented in the last 200 years) and legends about people who believe they have been abducted and subjected to intimate body examinations by aliens. Yet, in their varying ways, these and other 'folk beliefs' reflect the wide spectrum of belief and disbelief in what is easily dismissed as 'superstition'.

Explore Folklore provides a lively introduction to the study of most genres of British folklore, presenting the more contentious and profound ideas in a readily accessible manner.

ISBN 1 872883 60 5. Published 2002.
Perfect bound, demi 8vo (215x138 mm), 200 pages, **£9.95**

Also from Heart of Albion Press

Explore Green Men

Mercia MacDermott
with photographs by
Ruth Wylie

Explore Green Men is the first detailed study of the history of this motif for 25 years. Dr MacDermott's research follows the Green Man back from the previous earliest known examples into its hitherto unrecognised origins in India about 2,300 years ago.

The book starts by discussing the 'paganisation' of Green Men in recent decades, then follows backwards through the Victorian Gothic Revival, Baroque, Rococco and Italianate revivals, to their heyday in the Gothic and the supposed origins in the Romanesque. As part of this discussion there is background information on the cultural changes that affected how Green Men were regarded. The author also discusses the comparisons that have been made with Cernunnus, Robin Hood, Jack-in-the-Green, woodwoses, Baphomet, Al Khidr and Bulgarian *peperuda.* She also investigates which pagan god Green Men supposedly represent.

Explore Green Men is illustrated with 110 photographs and drawings, mostly of Green Men who have never before showed their faces in books.

This book will appeal to all with an interest in Green Men and to art historians looking for a reliable study of this fascinating decorative motif.

ISBN 1 872883 66 4. Published 2003.
Perfect bound, demi 8vo (215 x 138 mm), 216 pages, 108 b&w photos, 2 line drawings **£9.95**

Also from Heart of Albion Press

Footprints in Stone

The significance of foot- and hand-prints and other imprints left by early men, giants, heroes, devils, saints, animals, ghosts, witches, fairies and monsters

Janet Bord

From the earliest humans to the present day, there has always been a compulsion to 'leave one's mark': early cave art includes thousands of hand outlines, while many churches in Britain have foot outlines inscribed in lead and stone. These two extremes span almost 30,000 years during which time all kinds of persons, real and legendary, have left visible traces of themselves.

Most of the footprints – and hand-prints, knee-prints, and impressions of other body parts – are clearly not real, having allegedly been impressed into rocks around the world by such high-profile figures as the Buddha, Vishnu, Jesus Christ, and the Virgin Mary, as well as a vast panoply of saints, whose footprint traces and associated stories occupy two chapters. Their horses also left hoof-prints, and other animals are represented too. Not surprisingly, the ubiquitous Devil has a whole chapter to himself – but giants, villains and heroes, such as King Arthur, also feature strongly. Witches, fairies, ghosts and assorted spirits have made their mark: there are many modern instances of phantom hand- and foot-prints, the latter often bloodstained and indelible. Modern mysterious footprints are rarely graven in stone, but are rather more ephemeral, being left on the earth by monsters such as Bigfoot, or aliens who have briefly stepped out of their spacecraft. All these tales, old and new, may have some deeper meaning, and there is a chapter on the significance of footprints, as revealed in customs and folklore.

Hundreds of imprints are described in this book, which concludes with location details for more than 100 imprint sites all around the world.

ISBN 1 872883 73 7. Publishd 2004.
245 x 175 mm, 263 + x pages, 112 b&w photos, 26 line drawings, paperback. **£14.95**

Also from Heart of Albion Press

Stonehenge:
Celebration and Subversion

Andy Worthington

This innovative social history looks in detail at how the summer solstice celebrations at Stonehenge have brought together different aspects of British counter-culture to make the monument a 'living temple' and an icon of alternative Britain. The history of the celebrants and counter-cultural leaders is interwoven with the viewpoints of the land-owners, custodians and archaeologists who have generally attempted to impose order on the shifting patterns of these modern-day mythologies.

The story of the Stonehenge summer solstice celebrations begins with the Druid revival of the 18th century and the earliest public gatherings of the 19th and early 20th centuries. In the social upheavals of the 1960s and early 70s, these trailblazers were superseded by the Stonehenge Free Festival. This evolved from a small gathering to an anarchic free state the size of a small city, before its brutal suppression at the Battle of the Beanfield in 1985.

In the aftermath of the Beanfield, the author examines how the political and spiritual aspirations of the free festivals evolved into both the rave scene and the road protest movement, and how the prevailing trends in the counter-culture provided a fertile breeding ground for the development of new Druid groups, the growth of paganism in general, and the adoption of other sacred sites, in particular Stonehenge's gargantuan neighbour at Avebury.

The account is brought up to date with the reopening of Stonehenge on the summer solstice in 2000, the unprecedented crowds drawn by the new access arrangements, and the latest source of conflict, centred on a bitterly-contested road improvement scheme.

ISBN 1 872883 76 1. Published 2004. Perfect bound, 245 x 175 mm, 281 + xviii pages, 147 b&w photos, **£14.95**

Also from Heart of Albion Press

Snake Fat and Knotted Threads

An introduction to traditional Finnish healing magic

K.M. Koppana

What did the Finnish cunning man carry in his magic pouch? How does one learn the language of the ravens? What is the Origin of the Cat? How do you attract a partner at Midsummer? These and much more are to be found in *Snake Fat and Knotted Threads.*

Snake Fat and Knotted Threads provides a unique resource about traditional Finnish healing magic and spells, folk customs and myths. All this detailed information is based on the author's research and practical experience.

K.M. Koppana has been interested in spells since she was small, being a keen reader of fairy stories. This interest has persisted and she still has an urge to pick up pebbles on walks. She is also a poet and used to edit small magazines, such as the long-gone *Starlight,* which was about the Finnish magical scene. In 2001 she moved from Helsinki to England, settling in the Midlands.

> *Snake Fat and Knotted Threads* '... is a study of the *tietaja* or cunning folk who used such items as human skulls, graveyard dirt and hangmen's nooses in their magical work. They invoked both the old Finnish gods and Christian deities. This is a highly recommended study of a bygone era of magical belief that in modern Finland has been sadly usurped by New Age therapists and neo-pagan Goddess worship.'
> Michael Howard *The Cauldron*

1st UK edition published 2003 (originally published in Finland).
ISBN 1 872883 65 6 Perfect bound, demi 8vo, 112 pages, 14 b&w photos, 2 line drawings. **£7.95**

Also from Heart of Albion Press

Masterworks

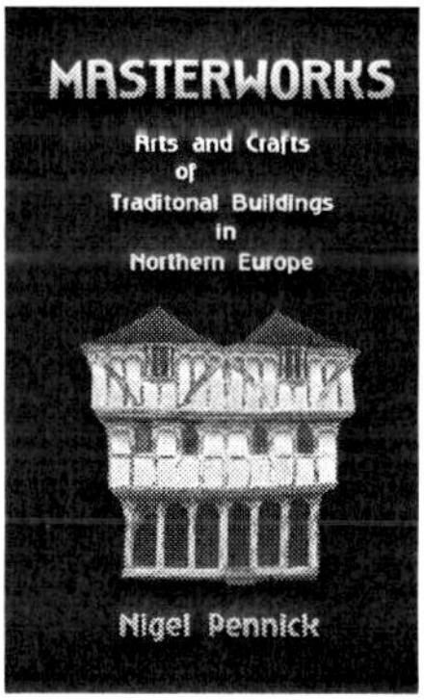

Arts and Crafts of Traditional Building in Northern Europe

Nigel Pennick

Masterworks is about the traditions of arts and crafts in northern Europe, taking as a starting point the use of timber in building. Timber frame buildings have been constructed over a long period of time over a large territory, mostly northern and north-west Europe. Various regional and local styles have come into being.

Timber buildings display a rich diversity of techniques, forms and patterns developed by generations of master craftsmen working with local materials under similar limitations. The 'arts and crafts' used in the construction of these buildings acknowledge and celebrate the knowledge, traditions, abilities and spiritual understanding of how to work effectively with natural materials. They are living traditions that remain relevant today.

Masterworks is a celebration of this arts and crafts ethos that is present in the traditional buildings of northern Europe.

> "*Masterworks* ... is written by a man who is not only in tune with his subject matter but is, in fact, a master wordsmith in his own right and deserves credit for this. I personally found this one of his most intriguing and important works to date and cannot recommend it too highly to the discerning reader."
>
> Ian Read *Runa*

ISBN 1 872883 63 X Publsihed 2002.
Perfect bound, Demi 8vo, 163 + viii pages, 23 b&w photos, 15 line drawings **£9.95**

Further details of all Heart of Albion titles online at
www.hoap.co.uk

All titles available direct from Heart of Albion Press.

Please add £1.30 p&p (UK only; email **albion@indigogroup.co.uk** for overseas postage).

To order books or request our current catalogue please contact

Heart of Albion Press

2 Cross Hill Close, Wymeswold

Loughborough, LE12 6UJ

Phone: 01509 880725

Fax: 01509 881715

email: albion@indigogroup.co.uk

Web site: www.hoap.co.uk